English Result

Intermediate Workbook

Joe McKenna

OXFORD
UNIVERSITY PRESS

1 Yourself and others

A How to **talk about the people in your life** » p.4

B How to **talk about greeting customs** » p.5

C How to **explain who people are** » p.6

D How to **correct a misunderstanding** » p.7

Skills Practice » pp.8–9

Self check 1 » p.76

2 Countries and cultures

A How to **talk about your background** » p.10

B How to **talk about tourism** » p.11

C How to **describe objects** » p.12

D How to **tell an anecdote** » p.13

Skills Practice » pp.14–15

Self check 2 » p.77

3 Learning and growing up

A How to **talk about your schooldays** » p.16

B How to **talk about your achievements** » p.17

C How to **offer hospitality** » p.18

D How to **talk about your education and career** » p.19

Skills Practice » pp.20–21

Self check 3 » p.78

4 Feelings and opinions

A How to **say how you feel about things** » p.22

B How to **talk about music** » p.23

C How to **compare and discuss preferences** » p.24

D How to **explain what a film is about** » p.25

Skills Practice » pp.26–27

Self check 4 » p.79

5 Law and order

A How to **talk about countries and governments** » p.28

B How to **talk about rules and laws** » p.29

C How to **talk about stories in the news** » p.30

D How to **talk about past events** » p.31

Skills Practice » pp.32–33

Self check 5 » p.80

6 Encounters

A How to **express strong feelings** » p.34

B How to **tell and show interest in an anecdote** » p.35

C How to **talk about people in your neighbourhood** » p.36

D How to **report what people said** » p.37

Skills Practice » pp.38–39

Self check 6 » p.81

7 Appearances

- **A** How to say how people look » p.40
- **B** How to talk about fashion » p.41
- **C** How to talk about plans and intentions » p.42
- **D** How to express guesses » p.43

  Skills Practice » pp.44–45

  Self check 7 » p.82

8 Communication

- **A** How to talk on the phone » p.46
- **B** How to talk about ability » p.47
- **C** How to report an interview » p.48
- **D** How to report a conversation » p.49

  Skills Practice » pp.50–51

  Self check 8 » p.83

9 Science and nature

- **A** How to make small talk » p.52
- **B** How to talk about your future » p.53
- **C** How to give advice » p.54
- **D** How to talk about unreal situations » p.55

  Skills Practice » pp.56–57

  Self check 9 » p.84

10 Shopping

- **A** How to exchange opinions » p.58
- **B** How to talk about your shopping habits » p.59
- **C** How to talk about recent activities » p.60
- **D** How to ask about products in a shop » p.61

  Skills Practice » pp.62–63

  Self check 10 » p.85

11 Travel

- **A** How to give and ask about directions » p.64
- **B** How to talk about holiday accommodation » p.65
- **C** How to give health advice » p.66
- **D** How to give extra information » p.67

  Skills Practice » pp.68–69

  Self check 11 » p.86

12 Stories

- **A** How to explain your point of view » p.70
- **B** How to talk about hopes and wishes » p.71
- **C** How to describe the plot of a story » p.72
- **D** How to talk about important decisions » p.73

  Skills Practice » pp.74–75

  Self check 12 » p.87

Self checks key » pp.88–90   **Audio scripts** » pp.91–94   **Irregular verbs** » p.95

How to talk about the people in your life

G subject questions and object questions   V the people in my life

1A

A Grammar subject and object questions

1 Underline the correct answer for each question.
   1 Who sang/did sing the song *I can't get you out of my head*?
   2 Who rescues Fiona/does rescue Fiona from a castle in the first *Shrek* film?
   3 Who won/did win the Formula 1 Motor Racing World Championship seven times?
   4 Who elect the French/do the French elect every five years?
   5 Who beat France/did beat France in the Football World Cup final in 2006?
   6 Who fought/did fight against Lord Voldemort?
   7 Who sent Russia/did Russia send into space in 1957?
   8 Who got/did get the most *Oscar* awards for Best Actress in her career?

2 Match these answers with the questions in exercise 1.
   ☐ their president
   ☐ Michael Schumacher
   ☐ Harry Potter
   ☐ Laika the dog
   ☑ Kylie Minogue
   ☐ Shrek
   ☐ Katharine Hepburn
   ☐ Italy

3 Write the correct questions for the information in **bold** below.
   1 **Derek and Maria** went to France last weekend.
      Who went to France last weekend?
   2 They wanted **a romantic break** in Paris.
      _____?
   3 They travelled by **Eurostar train** from London.
      _____?
   4 Derek left **his passport** on the train.
      _____?
   5 In Paris, **the immigration officials** sent them home.
      _____?
   6 **Maria** shouted at Derek all the way home.
      _____?
   7 They decided to go camping **in the back garden**.
      _____?
   8 **Their weekend** was very romantic in the end.
      _____?

B Vocabulary the people in my life

4 Add *a, e, i, o,* or *u* to complete the words.

family / marriage relationships	work / life relationships
__nt	*a*cq*u*_*a*_i nt*a*nc_*e*_
ncl	fl_tm_t_
n__c_	n__ghb__r
n_ph_w	b_st fr__nd
c__s_n	_x-b_yfr__nd /
br_th_r-_n-l_w	_x-g_rlfr__nd
st_pm_th_r	c_ll__g__
w_d_w / w_d_w_r	b_ss

5 Match the definitions with the correct words from exercise 4. Some definitions may match more than one word.
   1 A person you know, but not very well
      acquaintance
   2 The person at work who tells you what to do
      _____
   3 Your father's second wife _____
   4 A person you share a flat with _____
   5 Someone who works in the same place as you
      _____
   6 A person who lives next door _____
   7 Your husband or wife's brother _____
   8 Someone you used to go out with _____
   9 A person whose husband or wife has died
      _____

And you? Who are the people in your life? Write about relationships outside your immediate family.

My best friend is Carmen. We went to school together.

1
3
3
4
5

How well can you talk about the people in your life now?
Go back to the Student's Book >> p.7 and tick ✓ the line again.

How to **talk about greeting customs**

G reflexive pronouns **V** ways of greeting **P** *Miss* /s/ or *Ms* /z/

A Grammar reflexive pronouns

1 Match the sentences with the pictures.
1. [f] I was waiting by myself.
2. [ ] Can you do it yourself?
3. [ ] He's cooking for himself.
4. [ ] We'll carry them ourselves, thanks.
5. [ ] They're working by themselves.
6. [ ] They're talking to each other.

2 Complete these sentences with a suitable pronoun.
1. The children think they are old enough to go to the cinema by _themselves_.
2. On the first day of the course, we all had to introduce _____.
3. My sister is very good at sewing – she makes all her clothes _____.
4. You're 18 now, and you'll have to look after _____.
5. In army training, the soldiers practise by fighting _____.
6. The two climbers hurt _____ badly when they fell.
7. My friends always send _____ text messages at Christmas and New Year.
8. I couldn't find a teacher, so I had to study by _____.

B Vocabulary ways of greeting

3 Match the greeting actions with the parts of the body. Some parts of the body match more than one action.

actions	parts of the body
1 [c] shake	a whole body
2 [ ] bow	b arms
3 [ ] kiss	c hands
4 [ ] wave	d lips
5 [ ] hug	

4 Complete the sentences with a verb from exercise 3 in the correct tense.
1. The business people signed the papers and _shook_ hands.
2. It was time to leave, so the soldier and his girlfriend _____ each other.
3. Katie _____ her best friend when she felt upset.
4. The children _____ goodbye to their grandparents from the train window.
5. It's common in Japan to _____ to other people when you meet them.

C Pronunciation /s/ *Miss* or /z/ *Ms*

5 **1B.1** Listen and write *Miss*, *Ms*, *Mrs*, or *Mr* before the name.

1. _____ Wilson   5. _____ Brady
2. _____ Wilson   6. _____ Brady
3. _____ Wilson   7. _____ Brady
4. _____ Wilson   8. _____ Brady

And you? In your country, what is a typical greeting for these people? How would you greet them?

1. your grandparents
   I always hug my grandparents when I see them.
2. your best friend

3. your partner

4. a work colleague

5. a stranger

How well can you talk about greeting customs now?
Go back to the Student's Book >> p.9 and tick ✓ the line again.

How to explain who people are

G present simple and continuous   V position

A Grammar present simple and continuous

1 Underline the correct verb forms. Use the picture to help you.

OK Alice, this will be your new office, and these are your colleagues. That's Ms Walters in the corner. She's your new boss. She's here every day except Mondays, when she ¹*has* / *is having* meetings with the company directors. I ² *don't know* / *am not knowing* what they do in those meetings, but they certainly ³ *make* / *are making* a lot of noise!

The tall man over there is John. That's his desk on the left, but he ⁴ *makes* / *is making* photocopies at the moment. Then those are your two new colleagues in the middle: Brian on the left. He's the accountant – he ⁵ *manages* / *is managing* the company finances. Hmmm, he ⁶ *watches* / *is watching* football on the Internet at the moment! And opposite him is Jenny – she's the project manager. As you can see, she ⁷ *is* / *is being* pregnant, so she's leaving in March. Everyone ⁸ *works* / *is working* on a big project now, and we ⁹ *need* / *are needing* to finish it by the end of the month, so we're all quite busy. So, that's everyone. ¹⁰ *Do you have* / *Are you having* any questions?

2 Complete the conversation with the correct form of the verb in brackets. For some, both the present simple and present continuous are possible.

A So, tell me about your new neighbours.
B Well, I don't know much about them yet, but they're a young couple with a baby, and they ¹ _look_ (look) like nice people. Apparently, the wife works in the local hospital.
A Oh? Is she a doctor, then?
B No, I ² _____ (not think) so. Her husband said she ³ _____ (organize) the food and meals there, that sort of thing.
A Right. And what about him? ⁴ _____ (he work) at the hospital too?
B Well, he ⁵ _____ (not go) out to work at the moment.
A Why not?
B Because he ⁶ _____ (look after) their baby at home. They ⁷ _____ (have) a 10-month-old baby girl. She's very sweet.
A So what ⁸ _____ (he normally do) when he ⁹ _____ (not take care) of the family?
B Erm, I think he told me that he ¹⁰ _____ (be) some kind of technician.
A So, ¹¹ _____ (they make) a lot of noise?
B Well, the baby ¹² _____ (cry) a lot, of course. But they're quite quiet. They ¹³ _____ (not argue) much, for example. Not like the neighbours we had before. They shouted so much that we couldn't hear the TV!

B Vocabulary position

3 Complete the sentences with these prepositions.
~~at~~   in   behind   on   of   to   front

1 Alice's new boss sits _at_ the back of the office, _____ the right.   True / False
2 There is a door _____ the right of Ms Walters.   True / False
3 Brian is sitting in _____ of his computer at the moment.   True / False
4 John's desk is _____ the middle of the room, and _____ it is the office photocopier.   True / False
5 Ms Walters has got some books at the front _____ her desk.   True / False

4 Are the sentences in exercise 3 correct? Look again at the picture in exercise 1 and underline *True* or *False*.

And you? Describe:
1 what you're wearing now _____
2 what you wear to work / school _____
3 the clothes you wore to a recent party _____
4 the clothes you usually wear in summer _____

How well can you explain who people are now?
Go back to the Student's Book >> p.11 and tick ✓ the line again.

How to correct a misunderstanding

v cognates and false friends; misunderstandings   P the alphabet

A Vocabulary cognates and false friends

1 Translate these words into your language. Label them:
   C for cognates (similar spelling and meaning)
   F for false friends (similar spelling but different meaning)
   D for different (your word is spelt completely differently)

   television (n) _____
   arm (n) _____
   career (n) _____
   alphabet (n) _____
   orange (n) _____
   kind (adj) _____
   parcel (n) _____
   course (n) _____
   medicine (n) _____

2 Match the words with the pictures.

   1 [c] board   3 □ meat   5 □ piece   7 □ through
   2 □ guest   4 □ new   6 □ road   8 □ weight

3 Write the missing words. Then write the word in exercise 2 which sounds the same.

   1 past tense of 'ride' (vb)   rode   (road)
   2 past tense of 'know' (vb)   _____   (_____)
   3 past tense of 'throw' (vb)   _____   (_____)
   4 past tense of 'guess' (vb)   _____   (_____)
   5 not interested (adj)   _____   (_____)
   6 opposite of war (n)   _____   (_____)
   7 if your bus is late, you have to (vb) _____ (_____)
   8 when you (vb) _____ someone new, you say: 'How do you do?' (_____)

4 Complete the sentences with a suitable word from exercises 2 and 3.

   1 120 kilos! Oh dear, perhaps I should lose some _weight_.
   2 This statue is a symbol of _____ between our two countries.
   3 There's nothing to do in this town. We're so _____!
   4 I'm afraid the hotel is full. We only have space for 30 _____.
   5 The captain _____ into battle, and fell off his horse.
   6 What kind of _____ do you prefer: beef or chicken?
   7 During the argument, Sally _____ Dan's clothes, CDs, and laptop into the street.
   8 Ooh, I haven't seen those shoes before. Are they _____?

5 Complete the conversations with these phrases.
   I meant   I don't understand   I thought you said
   Oh, I see   ~~Pardon~~   I misunderstood

   A Can I see your papers, please?
   B ¹ _Pardon_ ?
   A Your papers.
   B Here you are.
   A No, not your newspaper! ² _____ your passport.
   B Sorry – ³ _____. Here it is.

   C We've got a lovely kitchen in our flat.
   D Oh really? I prefer beef, myself!
   C Beef? ⁴ _____!
   D Well, you said a lovely chicken, didn't you?
   C No, I didn't! I said *kitchen*!
   D ⁵ _____! Silly me! ⁶ _____ *chicken*!

B Pronunciation the alphabet

6 1D.1▶ Listen and circle the letter you hear.
   1 g / j   3 p / b   5 k / j   7 q / u   9 e / i
   2 s / z   4 t / d   6 i / y   8 m / n   10 a / e

7 1D.2▶ Listen and write the missing letters.
   1 _o_ _   5 _p_ _ _ _
   2 _hr_ _ _ _   6 co_ _ _ _ _ _
   3 _o_ t_ _ _   7 _u_ _ _ _ _
   4 _a_ _   8 la_ _ _ _ _ _

8 Check your answers in the audio script on >> p.91.

How well can you correct a misunderstanding now?
Go back to the Student's Book >> p.13 and tick ✓ the line again.

Unit 1 Skills Practice

A Read for detail

1 Where does this text come from?
   a ☐ a diary   b ☐ a novel   c ☐ a magazine

A life in pictures

1 Jethro Wiggins' photographs are currently on show at the *Expressions* Print Gallery. You might know that Jethro, 36, is the son of Duke Donald, lead singer of *The Pillbox Band*. He talked to us recently, here at *Dare* magazine, about the people in his life.

2 'A lot of people expected me to become a singer, like my father. He wasn't a great example, though. I hardly ever saw him when I was a child; he was always on tour with his band. I think my mother was disappointed in him too, because my parents got divorced when I was about ten.

3 'A few years later, my father remarried. My stepmother's a hairdresser. She didn't have any children of her own, so she spent a lot of time with me. She was just wonderful. We often went out to explore places, and she showed me how to use my first camera. She had a box full of her own photos. You know, artistic pictures, and that's what got me interested in photography.

4 'Friends? Well, I know my best friend Chris from our time at art college. We had a really good time there! He's a painter in Berlin now, but we keep in touch when we can. And there's Todd. He's just crazy. He works in a commercial photographic laboratory, but we spend time at weekends doing old-fashioned black-and-white developing. It's so different from modern digital work. And of course there's my girlfriend, Myriam. She's a model. We met when I was at a fashion magazine. She's the best thing that ever happened to me.'

2 Who do the paragraphs talk about? Write the paragraph number.
   a ☐ Jethro's friends   c ☐ Jethro's parents
   b ☐ Jethro himself   d ☐ Jethro's interest in photographs

3 Who are the people in Jethro's life? Match the names and the things he says about them.
   1 [e] father   a This person influenced my choice of career.
   2 ☐ mother   b We share a hobby.
   3 ☐ stepmother   c This is the most important person in my life.
   4 ☐ Chris   d I'd like to see this person more often.
   5 ☐ Todd   e ~~This person wasn't a very good parent.~~
   6 ☐ girlfriend   f This person probably wasn't very happy.

B Listen and follow a conversation

4 **1S.1▶** Listen to four conversations, 1–4. Match the conversations with situations a–d.

   a ☐ The wrong kind of clothes
   b ☐ A strange name
   c ☐ A shopping problem
   d ☐ A misunderstanding in the restaurant

5 Here is what the speaker intended. Write what the other person understood.
   1 shirt   *skirt*
   2 peas   _____
   3 soup   _____
   4 'H'   _____

6 Check your answers in the audio script on ▶▶ p.91.

8

C Read personal descriptions

7 Read the two descriptions quickly. What kind of Internet group are the people joining?
   a ☐ a group for jazz fans
   b ☐ a group for jazz musicians
   c ☐ a group for theatre-goers

---

www.jazzfriends.net

1 Our names are Harvey and Mariana. My husband Harvey's 54 and I'm 48. We live and work in Newcastle in the north of England. Harvey's family were originally from Jamaica, but they've been here for three generations now, and my family are all local too. Harvey was a widower when we first met, at a local theatre group. I'm a social worker by profession, but I've always loved acting.

2 Our other hobby is jazz. Harvey plays the trumpet – he's just the best! And I do a bit of singing. There's a great jazz club in town that we go to about twice a month.

3 We heard about this group at the club, and what we'd really like to do is make a music video and share it with you all on the Internet.

---

www.jazzfriends.net

1 My name's Ulrike and I'm 27 years old. I'm from Lübeck in Germany, but I live and work in Nagoya in central Japan. I've been here for three years now, and I must say that Japan is a fascinating place, although I miss my family and friends from home. We keep in touch by email.

2 I've listened to jazz music since I was a child. My father played jazz with a group of friends, and he was the pianist. I don't play an instrument myself, but I love the music.

3 I'm interested in joining this group because I have lots of good recordings to share, and a lot of questions to ask about classical jazz!

---

8 Both texts are organized in the same way. Match the paragraph numbers with the information below.
   a ☐ particular reasons for joining the group
   b ☐ self-introduction
   c ☐ general information about their interest in jazz

9 Tick ✓ the information you can find in both texts.
   ☐ abilities   ☐ jobs   ☐ where/live
   ☐ age   ☐ family   ☐ where/met partner
   ☐ interests

D Write a personal description

10 Read the email that Jamie wrote to an Internet group. Put the phrases in the correct place.

generous   neighbours   a bit of a disaster
birthday party   sense of humour

---

www.find-friends.com

Tell us about your best friend!

Hi everyone,

I'd like to introduce my best friend, Jackie.

As you can see from the photo, she's got long, dark hair and blue eyes. She's ¹_____ in real life! I mean, she's not very organized, but she's got a great ²_____. She makes me laugh all the time. And she's very ³_____. She always helps people out.

A lot of people meet their friends at school, I suppose, but I didn't. We met at my cousin's ⁴_____. Jackie and my cousin live in the same part of town. In fact, they're ⁵_____, so we often get together at my cousin's house, and then go out for the evening.

Anyway, that's my best friend. I can't wait to read all about yours!

Jamie

○ Uploaded image

---

11 Make some notes about Jamie's friend, and about your best friend.

	Jackie	Your friend
Appearance		
Character		
Where / How met		
Where / When see each other		

12 Write an email to introduce your best friend.

_____
_____
_____
_____
_____
_____
_____

13 Review your writing. Underline any changes you could make.

Now try the Self check on >> p.76.

9

How to talk about your background

G *the* before geographical names **V** people and places **P** spelling and pronunciation: *c* and *g*

A Grammar *the* before geographical names

1 Match the names with the geographical features.
1 [d] Andes, Sierra Madre — a continent
2 [ ] Orizaba — b ocean
3 [ ] Pacific — c lake
4 [ ] Caribbean — d mountain range
5 [ ] Maracaibo — e desert
6 [ ] Orinoco, Mississippi — f island group
7 [ ] Sonora — g sea
8 [ ] South America — h rivers
9 [ ] West Indies — i mountain

2 Write *the* or nothing before the names.
1 *The* Andes are in _____ South America.
2 _____ Sonora Desert, _____ Mount Orizaba and _____ Sierra Madre Mountains are in _____ Mexico.
3 _____ Lake Maracaibo and _____ Orinoco River are in _____ Venezuela.
4 _____ West Indies is a group of islands between _____ Caribbean Sea and _____ Atlantic Ocean.
5 _____ Mississippi River is in _____ United States.

3 Complete the labels on the map with places from exercise 1. Use the sentences in exercise 2 to help you.

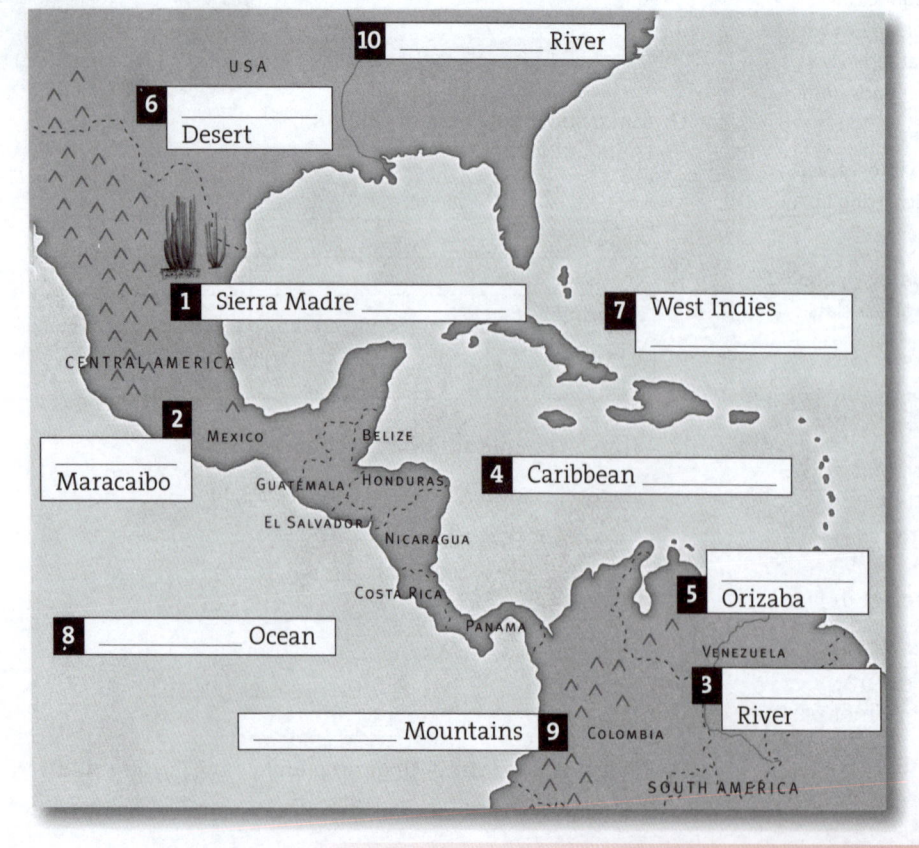

Map labels:
- 10 _____ River
- USA
- 6 _____ Desert
- 1 Sierra Madre _____
- 7 West Indies _____
- CENTRAL AMERICA
- 2 _____ Maracaibo
- MEXICO, BELIZE, GUATEMALA, HONDURAS, EL SALVADOR, NICARAGUA, COSTA RICA, PANAMA
- 4 Caribbean _____
- 8 _____ Ocean
- 5 _____ Orizaba
- VENEZUELA, COLOMBIA
- 3 _____ River
- 9 _____ Mountains
- SOUTH AMERICA

B Vocabulary people and places

4 Complete the sentences with a country, region or religion.
1 G*u* *a*tem*a* *l*a is a country in C*e* ntral A*m* *eri*ca.
2 B_l____a is a country in S__th A_____a.
3 T__z__ia is a country in E____ Af___a.
4 The _us__m religion is common in the M__d__ E_s_.
5 The C_r____ian and J__is_ religions began in the ____le __st.
6 There are many islands in the S____h P__if__.
7 The coast of Ea__ Af__ca is on the I__ia_ O____n.

C Spelling and Pronunciation: *c* and *g*

5 Put the words in the correct column.
~~golden~~ ~~city~~ ~~region~~ games ~~typical~~
central face egg place together
marriage costume Atlantic fact
bag Germany

The letter c	
/s/	/k/
city	typical

The letter g	
/dʒ/	/g/
region	golden

6 **2A.1** Listen and repeat.

How well can you talk about your background now?
Go back to the Student's Book >> p.17 and tick ✓ the line again.

How to talk about tourism

G adverbs of frequency   P adverbs of frequency

A Grammar adverbs of frequency

1 Number the adverbs from most frequent (*1*) to least frequent (*7*).
- [1] always
- [ ] hardly ever
- [ ] never
- [ ] often
- [ ] rarely
- [ ] sometimes
- [ ] usually

2 Underline the correct adverb. Use the hotel activity programme to help you.

HOTEL PARADIS TROPIQUE
Torquay

Sports & exercise
WATER POLO — *daily, 11.00–12.00*
AEROBICS — *daily, 8.30–9.30*
TAI CHI — *Sat., Sun. 11.00–12.00*
HORSE RIDING — *Available June–Sept*

Social
BINGO — *daily, 19.00–20.00 (winter only)*
DISCOTHEQUE — *Fri., Sat., Sun., 22.00*
KARAOKE CLUB — *most Fridays (ask at reception)*

Excursions
SHOPPING TRIPS — *daily, 9.00, 13.00*
ARTS VILLAGE — *2nd Wed. of month*
MOUNTAIN WALKS — *summer only; minimum groups of 20*

Cultural
LOCAL COOKING CLASSES — *No longer available*
ILLUSTRATED TALKS — *1st & 3rd Wed. of month*

1 You can <u>always</u>/sometimes go on shopping trips.
2 They sometimes/never have excursions to the arts village.
3 They sometimes/never offer horse riding in winter.
4 They usually/hardly ever organize mountain walks in summer.
5 They always/sometimes play bingo in winter.
6 They usually/rarely have karaoke in summer.
7 You can rarely/often go to an illustrated talk.
8 They always/sometimes do tai chi at the weekends.
9 You can never/hardly ever do local cooking classes.

3 Correct the sentences.
1 We not often go on holiday abroad.
   We don't often go on holiday abroad.
2 My cousin goes usually on a camping holiday.
   _____.
3 Marco hardly never does any sightseeing.
   _____.
4 My grandparents always have travelled first class.
   _____.
5 I sometimes am ill when I fly.
   _____.

B Pronunciation adverbs of frequency

4 **2B.1** Listen and write the adverbs of frequency.

MY TRAVELLING AUNT

She says she ¹_____ goes
To the places that she knows.
But the food, she ²_____ tries
If the restaurant's won a prize.
And you can ³_____ see her queue
For tickets to somewhere new.

She ⁴_____ hires a car
The monuments aren't that far.
She ⁵_____ takes the bus
Sits with locals just like us.
Quite ⁶_____, she'll stop and chat
To find out where you're at.

⁷_____, she even stops for tea
But she ⁸_____ writes to me!

The alternative tourist

5 Listen again and repeat. Are the adverbs of frequency stressed?

And you? What kind of tourist are you? Complete the sentences, using some of the verbs below.

go to   have   learn   remember   take   visit   write

1 I never _____.
2 I sometimes _____.
3 I don't often _____.
4 I always _____.
5 I usually _____.

How well can you talk about tourism now?
Go back to the Student's Book >> p.19 and tick ✓ the line again.

How to describe objects

v words and phrases for describing objects   p stress of prepositions

A Vocabulary phrases for describing objects

1 Read the descriptions quickly and match them with the pictures.

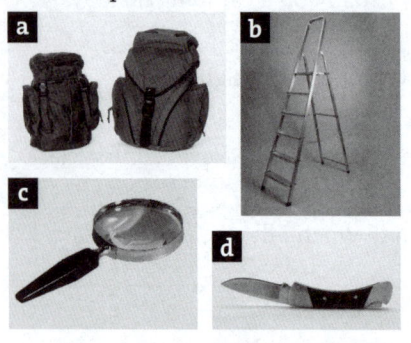

a   b   c   d

1 ☐ It's ¹ _made of_ metal and has a wooden handle. It's short when it's closed. It's ² _used as_ a tool when we go on trips.

2 ☐ It's usually ³_____ metal, but it can also be wood. It's very tall and flat. The ends are often ⁴_____ rubber, so it can stand up safely. It's ⁵_____ a way of getting to high places.

3 ☐ It's a ⁶_____ bag. It's made of cloth and nylon, and you can use the straps to wear it on your back. It's got a lot of pockets on the sides. It can be ⁷_____ carrying sports clothes, or school books.

4 ☐ It's a round piece of glass, with a frame to protect the glass. The frame could be metal or plastic. You use it to see small things more clearly. It ⁸_____ a small plate with a handle.

2 Complete the descriptions in exercise 1 with these phrases.
covered with   kind of   looks like   made of ×2
used as ×2   used for

3 Complete the table with the words from exercise 1. Use a dictionary if you need to.
~~metal~~ wood ends tall flat cloth ~~short~~
nylon straps pockets sides small round
glass ~~handle~~ frame plastic

material (n)	shape and size (adj)	parts of an object (n)
metal	short	handle

4 Tick ✓ the correct sentences. Sometimes both options are correct.

1 a ☐ A briefcase looks like a small suitcase.
  b ☐ A briefcase is used as a small suitcase.
2 a ☐ A wallet is used for carrying money.
  b ☐ A wallet is used as carrying money.
3 a ☐ A jacket is a kind of coat.
  b ☐ A jacket is used as a kind of coat.

B Pronunciation stress of prepositions

5 2C.1▶ Listen and write the prepositions you hear.
as   for   from   of

1 ☐ _as_   5 ☐ _____
2 ☐ _____   6 ☐ _____
3 ☐ _____   7 ☐ _____
4 ☐ _____   8 ☐ _____

6 Listen again and tick ✓ the prepositions that are stressed.

And you? Imagine you lost two of the items below while on a train journey, but you don't know the word for them in English. Describe them to the person at the lost property office.

a suitcase   an umbrella   a wallet   a purse
a jacket   a briefcase

1

2

How well can you describe objects now?
Go back to the Student's Book >> p.21 and tick ✓ the line again.

12

How to **tell an anecdote**

G past simple and past continuous   V time expressions

A Grammar past simple and past continuous

BY BUS IN JAVA

1 Match the sentences with the pictures.
1 [c] We were getting on the bus and it left.
2 ☐ We got on the bus and it left.
3 ☐ We crossed a river and we took photos.
4 ☐ We were crossing a river and we took photos.
5 ☐ We were getting off the bus and we fell.
6 ☐ We got off the bus and we fell.

2 Underline the correct words.

Ellis and I [1] looked for / were looking for a restaurant when the rain [2] started / was starting, so we [3] stopped / were stopping in the nearest one. It was quite busy, so we [4] had to / were having to share a table with an old couple. We [5] ordered / were ordering the food and [6] had / were having a drink while we were waiting. When the food [7] arrived / was arriving, I was very hungry, and I started eating immediately. Suddenly I noticed the other couple [8] looked / were looking at me – and I think they [9] were / were being quite unhappy. Then Ellis [10] told / was telling me what was wrong: I [11] ate / was eating with my left hand, and this is something you should never do in Muslim countries!

3 Put the sentences in order (1–8) to complete the tale.
a ☐ The hotel owner asked us for our passports, but we didn't have them with us!
b ☐ We went there by bus. When we arrived, we went to find a hotel.
c [1] Ellis and I were travelling in Java when this story happened.
d ☐ He said we couldn't stay at the hotel without passports, but we could sleep at the police station if we wanted!
e ☐ After that experience, we never forgot to take our passports whenever we went travelling.
f ☐ The policeman explained that all foreigners had to carry their passports with them all the time.
g ☐ One day we decided to visit a town, where they were celebrating a festival.
h ☐ While we were all talking, a policeman arrived.

B Vocabulary time expressions

4 Complete another tale with the time expressions in the box.

after   during   finally   for   later   next   when ×2

I'm from the west of Ireland, originally. [1] _When_ I finished university, I decided to leave Ireland to find work. Although I missed home, I enjoyed living in London for a while. But [2] _____ two years, I felt I needed a change, so I bought a ticket to Ecuador, a country that many of my friends were talking about. Two months [3] _____, I was in Quito, a beautiful city high up in the mountains. First, I explored the city. [4] _____, I decided to walk on the old Inca Trail, the Camino Real. It was hard work, but the views were just wonderful. [5] _____ the walk, some clouds came down and it was difficult to see. Then I heard this magical Irish music. It reminded me of home. [6] _____ a while, I thought I was dreaming! I just couldn't believe it. The day after that, [7] _____ I came down for breakfast at my hotel, I [8] _____ discovered the truth. Someone was practising Irish music in the hotel gardens. It was an American tourist who was making the magical music of home!

And you? What happened in your life yesterday? Complete the sentences.

1 After I got up, _____.
2 While I was waiting for the bus/train, _____.
3 During the journey, _____.
4 Half an hour later, _____.
5 In the end, _____.

How well can you tell an anecdote now?
Go back to the Student's Book >> p.23 and tick ✓ the line again.

Unit 2 Skills Practice

A Read for detail

1 What kind of text is this?
   a ☐ an anecdote
   b ☐ a letter
   c ☐ a magazine article

1 Of all the exotic traditions on the planet, the neck coils worn by the women of South-East Asia must be one of the most unusual.

2 These women belong to the Padaung people, a small ethnic group of about 7,000 people who live in northern Thailand. The women start wearing the neck coils at about the age of five. As they grow older, they add more coils. The weight of the metal pushes the shoulders down, and this gives the impression of a very long neck. It's possible to take the coils off, but that doesn't happen very often, because it is very uncomfortable.

3 There are many stories relating to the origins of this custom. Some say that the coils once protected the women from slavery, or were worn to guard against tiger attacks. Others say that they were worn as a sign of beauty and wealth. In the past, men who were looking for a wife chose the women with the best coils. But perhaps the most interesting story is the origin-myth of the Padaung people. This story says that Man was the wind, and Woman was a beautiful, long-necked dragon. When the dragon was flying through the sky, the wind fell in love with her, and the Padaung people were born from the union of the two. Ever since then, the women of the tribe have worn the coils, in memory of their dragon-mother.

2 Write the paragraph number next to the ideas.
   a ☐ why the women use the coils
   b ☐ introducing the topic
   c ☐ how the coils work

3 Correct the facts in these sentences.
   1 The Padaung people live in southern Thailand.
      The Padaung people live in northern Thailand.
   2 Women are fifteen when they start wearing neck coils.
      _____
   3 As the women get older, the coils become lighter.
      _____
   4 They take off the coils at night, when they want to sleep.
      _____
   5 The text mentions five stories about the origin of the coils.
      _____
   6 In the past, men chose women with the most coils.
      _____
   7 The wind found the dragon on a mountain top.
      _____
   8 The women wear the coils to remember the wind.
      _____

B Listen for detail

4 25.1▶ Listen and write *M* for Maggie or *G* for Gerry.
   1 [M] is home for Christmas.
   2 ☐ has been in South Asia.
   3 ☐ works in Spain.
   4 ☐ had a problem greeting people.
   5 ☐ had a problem understanding people.
   6 ☐ says that it would be a problem for everyone.

5 Listen again and then correct these phrases.
   1 I didn't see you for a very long time.
   2 When you see people, you touch them on the cheeks.
   3 Ask what the other people do, and then just do the opposite.
   4 They shake their arms to say *no*, and nod their heads to say *yes*.

6 Listen and check.

7 Translate the corrected phrases from exercise 5 into your own language.

C Read a travel blog

8 Match paragraphs 1–5 to topics a–e.
- a ☒5 Recommendations for visitors
- b ☐ What happened after lunch
- c ☐ The temple
- d ☐ Getting there
- e ☐ What happened at lunch

1 It was a hot, sunny day when we decided to visit Gharapuri (also known as Elephanta). The trip took half an hour and cost about 250 rupees. During the crossing, we saw a lot of big ships going to and from Mumbai, so we often felt quite small on the ferry! When we got to the island, we had to climb lots and lots of steps up to the temple. So then we rested at the entrance and drank some water. Twenty minutes later, we went inside.

2 The first thing we noticed was the temperature. I mean, the temple is like a big cave cut out of the rock, so it's much cooler than outside. And it isn't very light, so at first you can't see properly. Then you see this enormous sculpture with three heads. The guide book says these are the three aspects of the Hindu god Shiva. Amazing! We visited the rest of the temple, and then looked for somewhere to have lunch.

3 We found a quiet place under a big tree and got our sandwiches out. Then three or four monkeys appeared. My brother took a photo – and the monkey took his sandwich! Next, another one stole some fruit we had near the bags, so we chased the monkeys away. In the end, we finished eating quite quickly.

4 Afterwards, we climbed the hill to see the views from the top. We sat down to rest. The weather was still warm, and we fell asleep. When we woke up, it was much cooler, so we ran back to the ferry stop. But the last ferry leaves at six, and it was nearly seven o'clock. And that's how we discovered that there's nowhere to sleep on the island: we had to sleep under a tree!

5 Anyway, Gharapuri is a fantastic place to visit. Just remember these two things: don't eat in front of the monkeys, because they're a real pest. And don't miss the last ferry back to Mumbai!

9 Complete these notes a traveller made after reading the blog.

Day trips from Mumbai
To: [1]_____ Island
Transport: by [2]_____
Cost: [3]_____
Duration of ferry crossing: [4]_____ hour
What to see and do: [5]_____
What not to do: [6]_____

D Write a travel story

10 Look at these paragraph topics. How would you organize them in a travel story? Write 1–4. Read the paragraphs below quickly to check your answer.
- a ☐ seeing the sights
- b ☐ getting there
- c ☐ food and accommodation
- d ☐ a transport problem

1 Five of us went off to Amsterdam late last summer for a week. We finished our holiday jobs, and we thought we deserved a break. We got a cheap flight to Amsterdam, took a bus into town, and went to see the sights.

2 None of us knew the place, so it was a bit of an adventure, and we got completely lost at one point. My friend Dave nearly fell into a canal [1] *when we were crossing a bridge* because he wasn't looking where he was going! But we managed to find the Van Gogh museum, where we had to queue for two hours. There were so many people! [2]_____ , I met an old friend from school. The world's a small place!

3 We stayed in a travellers' hostel, and met some friendly Italians [3]_____. The hostel was cheap and clean, although you have to be very tidy. Ten people in one dormitory can be a problem! And for food, we generally ate in fast food places. Did you know the Dutch have mayonnaise with their chips? But on my birthday we had a special big meal at an Indonesian restaurant. [4]_____ after that when my best mate Billy lost his camera. Poor Billy, he was really annoyed.

4 Anyway, public transport is good, so it's easy to get around the city. A lot of people rent bikes, but we preferred to go by bus. You have to be careful though. You get your ticket from a machine, not from the driver. [5]_____ on Friday, two of the boys didn't have any money to buy a ticket, and an inspector caught them. They had to pay five times the fare! They tried to say they were foreigners, but the man didn't accept that. The rest of us just laughed. In the end, we all had a great time and would love to go back to Holland.

11 Complete the text in exercise 10 by putting these phrases in the correct places.
- a we were having a drink
- b while we were waiting there
- c when we were going to the Vondelpark
- d ~~when we were crossing a bridge~~
- e who were staying there too

12 Prepare to write your own travel story. Use these questions to make notes before you write.
1. How did you get there?
2. What did you see and do while you were there?
3. Describe a specific incident that you remember.
4. What did you think of the whole experience?

13 Now write your travel story.

Now try the Self check on >> p.77.

15

How to talk about your schooldays

G used to   V school words   P rhythm

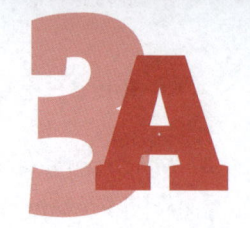

A Grammar used to

1 Underline *used to* where you can use this instead of the past simple. If not, underline the correct option.

> My primary school building doesn't exist any more. It was so old that they ¹built/used to build a new one twenty years ago. But I still remember it very clearly, because I ²went/used to go there for six whole years.
>
> It always ³looked/used to look very big to us, but of course we were much smaller then! There were separate doors for boys and girls, but we didn't really ⁴go/use to go in that way – everyone ⁵went/used to go in through the main door.
>
> The toilets were outside and it was always cold, so we only ⁶went/used to go in an emergency! There was a big concrete playground, but it was broken in many places, and one day a boy ⁷broke/used to break his ankle when he ⁸fell/used to fall on it.
>
> The school ⁹didn't have/didn't use to have a gymnasium or anything like that. We ¹⁰did/used to do exercises in the assembly area. I must say that I ¹¹wasn't/didn't use to be very upset when I finally ¹²left/used to leave the school!

2 Rewrite the sentences using a suitable form of *used to*.

1 I travelled 30 km to high school every day.
   I used to travel 30 km to high school every day.

2 I didn't like the journey in winter.
   _____.

3 How did you get to school?
   _____?

4 I took the number 19 bus.
   _____.

5 Did you have your meals in the canteen?
   _____?

6 Yes, but they weren't very good.
   _____.

7 Did you always do your homework?
   _____?

8 I did most of it on the bus!
   _____.

B Vocabulary school words

3 Complete the crossword.

Across
5 A subject taught in a laboratory that often involves experiments
6 A kind of table that pupils use
8 Daily or weekly meeting of all teachers and pupils in a school
10 Written exercises students do outside the school
11 The place at school where you have meals

Down
1 What the teacher writes the lesson on with chalk
2 The name for a child attending school
3 The person responsible for the whole school (male form of word)
4 Free time between classes
7 The area within the school grounds where pupils can play
9 A school subject that involves numbers, shapes and calculations

C Pronunciation rhythm

4 Put the phrases in the column with the correct stress pattern.

~~top of the class~~   ~~took the bus~~   finally met   ~~lunch break~~
childhood dreams   French class   teacher's pet

••	••	•••
lunch break	took the bus	top of the class

5 3A.1▶ Listen, and repeat.

How well can you talk about your schooldays now?
Go back to the Student's Book >> p.27 and tick ✓ the line again.

How to talk about your achievements

G present perfect and past simple   V achievement words

A Grammar present perfect and past simple

1 Underline the correct words in Linda's letter. Sometimes more than one answer is possible.

Denver
2nd February

Dear Mum and Dad,
It ¹ was / has been good to hear from you last week. We're in the middle of a Denver winter right now, and the children think it's wonderful. We ² never saw / have never seen this much snow in our lives before! It ³ snowed / has snowed so much last week that the school was closed for three days.

Marta's better now, but she ⁴ went / has been to the doctor at the weekend with a high fever. Brian's still enjoying his job. His car ⁵ broke / has broken down yesterday, so he ⁶ took / has taken it to the garage, and he ⁷ borrowed / has borrowed mine until the end of the week. I keep telling him that he ⁸ didn't have / hasn't had enough exercise since we arrived here last March.

I can't believe that we ⁹ were / have been here for nearly a year now! Take care, and write soon with your news. Or give me a call. We ¹⁰ didn't talk / haven't talked on the phone for ages!

Love,
Linda

2 Write the correct form of the verbs in Mum's letter. Sometimes more than one answer is possible.

Plymouth
17th February

Dear Linda,
Thanks for your letter with all your news. It only ¹ (arrive) _arrived_ in the post yesterday, probably because we ² (have) _____ a lot of bad weather recently too. We ³ (not get) _____ any post at all for most of last week!

Are you anywhere near Yellowstone Park? Your Dad and I ⁴ (be) _____ a bit worried since we ⁵ (read) _____ an article in the paper last Sunday. The report ⁶ (say) _____ that scientists ⁷ (find) _____ a lot of volcanic activity in the park. The last explosion there ⁸ (happen) _____ a long time ago, but they're not very sure of what's happening now. ⁹ (you hear) _____ anything about that? It wouldn't affect you in Denver, would it? Anyway, nothing much ¹⁰ (happen) _____ here since my last letter.

I must go now and get the shopping done.
All our love,
Mum

3 Do the following sentences refer to finished or unfinished time? Write *f* (finished) or *u* (unfinished) in the box.
1 ☐ We had an awful lot of snow last week.
2 ☐ Marta has felt better this week.
3 ☐ I sent the letter yesterday.
4 ☐ Brian has used the car a lot since he started his new job.

B Vocabulary achievement words

4 Match the sentence halves.
1 [c] How many times have you given up
2 ☐ It was 11 p.m. before Tim managed
3 ☐ We're all in a hurry!
4 ☐ I passed my Maths exam, but
5 ☐ If I fail the course,
6 ☐ Come on! You mustn't

a give up now!
b failed Physics.
c ~~smoking?~~
d can I try again?
e to finish his homework.
f Can you keep moving?

5 Complete the sentences with the correct form of these words.

achieve   succeed

1 He's always wanted to _achieve_ fame and fortune.
2 We wish you every _success_ in your new job!
3 If Hunt _____ in this race, he's won the championship.
4 Fleming's greatest _____ was the discovery of penicillin.
5 If they _____ in finding a cure for cancer, they'll win a Nobel prize.
6 The boys have cooked dinner – but they haven't been very _____!

And you? Answer the questions about *your* achievements.

1 What has been your greatest personal achievement?

2 What other ambitions have you succeeded in?

3 What would you like to achieve in the future?

How well can you talk about your achievements now?
Go back to the Student's Book >> p.29 and tick ✓ the line again.

17

How to offer hospitality

G phrasal verbs   V phrasal verbs; hospitality phrases

A Grammar phrasal verbs

1 Underline the correct words.
 1 Put away your clothes/Put away before we leave!
 2 Yes, I do yoga. The doctor told me to take up it/take it up after my accident.
 3 It's hot in here! Could you turn the fan on/turn on, please?
 4 The bus leaves in five minutes! We need to hurry us up/hurry up!
 5 She wanted to ask a question, but he just carried on speaking/carried speaking on.
 6 The workers were late and the boss told off them/told them off.

2 Complete the sentences with the correct form of the verbs in brackets. You may need to add a pronoun.
 1 Is this story true, or did you _make it up_? (make up)
 2 Have you _____ your room yet? (tidy up)
 3 They missed the bus because they _____ in time! (not wake up)
 4 What do you want to be when you _____? (grow up)
 5 Are these your books? I asked you an hour ago to _____. (put away)
 6 This isn't your jacket! _____ immediately! (take off)

B Vocabulary phrasal verbs; hospitality phrases

3 Answer the questions using the correct form of one of these phrasal verbs.

 carry on   take up   ~~put on~~   wash up   turn up

 1 You bought a new pair of jeans on Saturday and you wore them that evening. What did you do?
  I put on my new jeans on Saturday evening.
 2 You cleared the table after lunch. What did you do with the dishes?
  _____.
 3 You were reading a book when the phone rang. After the phone call, what did you do?
  _____.
 4 You can't hear the radio properly, so what are you doing?
  _____.
 5 You're bored with tennis, but golf looks interesting. What will you do?
  _____.

4 Complete the text with these particles.
 away   down   off ×2   on ×2   up ×2

Sharon was going to visit her grandfather, but the bus was late, and the journey was so slow. 'Oh, hurry [1] _up_ !' she thought. But the bus carried [2] _____ like it always did, stopping every 200 metres for new passengers. She was so tired that she fell asleep during the journey. Fortunately, she woke [3] _____ just in time to get off at the right stop.
 When she arrived at her grandfather's flat, she took her jacket [4] _____ and sat [5] _____ in an armchair. 'Give me your coat – I'll put it [6] _____ for you,' said her grandfather. 'Shall I make you some tea? Help yourself to the cakes.' Sharon could never resist cakes. 'I remember when your mother used to tell you [7] _____ for eating too many,' laughed Grandfather. 'But she's not here just now. Why don't you switch [8] _____ the light? It's getting dark.' Sharon finally began to relax. Grandfather's was her favourite place in the world.

5 Correct the sentences.
 1 I make you a cup of tea, if you like.
  I'll make you a cup of tea, if you like.
 2 Let the washing up. I'll do it.
  _____.
 3 Would you like that I make dinner?
  _____.
 4 Why don't you to turn on the TV?
  _____.
 5 Help you to more cake.
  _____.
 6 Is all right with the meal?
  _____.

How well can you offer hospitality now?
Go back to the Student's Book ›› p.31 and tick ✓ the line again.

How to **talk about your education and career** 3D

v education **p** word endings which can affect stress

A Vocabulary education

1 Match these UK qualifications with definitions a–e.
1. ☐ 'A' level
2. ☐ Degree
3. ☐ Doctorate
4. ☐ GCSE
5. ☐ Master's degree

a You take this exam after the minimum five years of secondary school.
b You do these exams after a sixth and seventh year at secondary school.
c This is the basic university qualification, usually awarded after a three-year course.
d This is a second-level university qualification, which you receive after a one- or two-year course.
e The highest qualification you can receive from a university.

2 Write these definitions correctly.
1. University department, e.g. of Arts / Law / Medicine / Science cuatlyf _faculty_
2. University classes steelruc _____
3. to complete all your university studies dragetua _____
4. top university teacher sporrefos _____
5. not as big as a university eleclog _____
6. to finish both studying and training yafiluq _____

3 Complete the sentences with a word from exercise 2.
1. She's doing a language degree in the _faculty_ of Arts.
2. You can only _____ as an architect after studying for up to seven years.
3. Afternoon _____ are so boring! I prefer to work in the library.
4. Excuse me. I'm looking for _____ Hamilton, from the Chemistry Department.
5. I'm hoping to _____ from university next year and find a job as soon as possible.
6. She's studying at a further education _____, and she'd like to teach Art.

B Pronunciation word endings which can affect stress

4 3D.1▶ Listen to the words. Tick ✓ if you hear one of these endings.

-tion -ogy -ity -aphy -istry

1 ☐ 6 ☐
2 ☐ 7 ☐
3 ☐ 8 ☐
4 ☐ 9 ☐
5 ☐ 10 ☐

5 Check your answers in the audio script on >> p.91. Listen and repeat the words.

And you? Write about your own education and training.

1 At primary school, I…
_____.
2 At secondary school, I…
_____.
3 I enjoyed / didn't enjoy school because…
_____.
4 I finished / will finish school at the age of…
_____.
5 After finishing school, I…
_____.
6 Now I…
_____.

How well can you talk about your education and career now?
Go back to the Student's Book >> p.33 and tick ✓ the line again.

Unit 3 Skills Practice

A Read and answer a questionnaire

1 Do the hospitality questionnaire. Then check your score and read your results. Do they surprise you?

What would *you* say in these situations?

1 Your cousin and his family of five want to come and stay for a week.

a *We haven't seen them for ages. It'll be good to talk.*
b *I hope we manage to keep them busy.*
c *The last time they came, our dogs ran away!*

2 Your 16-year-old son brings his school football team home for lunch.

a *He's crazy!*
b *Well, it's the first time he's brought his friends home.*
c *He didn't use to be so sociable!*

3 It's 2 a.m. and your party guests haven't gone home yet.

a *I'm going to go to bed in a minute.*
b *If he carries on telling stories, I'll fall asleep!*
c *We've had a great evening, but I do have to get up at seven!*

4 Your friends' children refuse to eat the food you have prepared.

a *I'm afraid there's nothing else, really.*
b *Shall I make them a sandwich?*
c *I could drive them to the café in town.*

5 Your parents-in-law come to visit, and there aren't enough beds.

a *Why don't you sleep in our bed?*
b *The sofa in the front room is really very comfortable.*
c *I'll book you a room in the hotel across the road, if you like.*

6 Foreign friends have arrived unexpectedly. You have an important meeting at work.

a *I won't be long. Help yourselves to food and drink.*
b *If you have any problems, just ask the neighbours.*
c *Why don't you go for a walk until about five o'clock?*

Read your results

9–12 You are an excellent host/hostess. It would be a pleasure to visit you!
5–8 You have some good ideas, but you probably need to do more.
0–4 You have a lot to learn about living with other people! Have you thought about taking lessons in hospitality?!

Check your score

	a	b	c
Question 1	2	1	0
Question 2	0	2	1
Question 3	0	1	2
Question 4	0	1	2
Question 5	2	0	1
Question 6	0	1	2

B Listen to school memories

2 **3S.1▶** Match the speakers 1–4 with the countries.
☒ France ☐ Germany ☐ Britain ☐ Spain

3 Write the speaker's number next to their experiences.

a _2_ didn't enjoy the food.
b ___ played sports at school.
c ___ went to school by bicycle.
d ___ was sometimes hit by the teachers.
e ___ slept at school during the week.
f ___ studied, but didn't learn about real life.
g ___ did a lot of exams twice.
h ___ didn't enjoy studying languages.

C Read for the main points

4 Answer the questions.
1. Which speaker from exercise 2 wrote the text below?
   _____

2. What is the text about? Tick ✓ the correct answer.
   a ☐ a CV
   b ☐ an application for a course
   c ☐ a newspaper article about stress at work

Dear Sir or Madam,

1. I read your advertisement in the *Daily Blurb* this morning, and I would like to apply for a place on the four-week course in conflict management.

2. I am 35 years old and I graduated from the University of Berlin with a first-class degree in Chemistry, as you can see from the enclosed CV. I then studied English and completed my doctorate at Manchester University.

3. For the next four years I worked for an important European chemical company. I used to enjoy my work but the company was very competitive, so the job became stressful. People used to argue all the time. I decided to find a more satisfying job, and took up teaching. In my current job, I still have to deal with difficult colleagues and students. I feel that the course you offer would be very helpful for this. I also think I could contribute a lot, from my own work experience.

4. I would be very grateful if you could send me an application form and full details of the course, including the cost.

I look forward to hearing from you soon,

Yours faithfully,

U. Kramer

---

5 Match paragraphs 1–4 in the letter with the writer's intentions.
   a ☐ giving her reasons for applying
   b ☐ saying how she heard about the course
   c ☐ saying what her qualifications are
   d ☐ asking for more information

D Write a CV

6 Complete the headings A–E in the CV with these phrases.
Education   Interests   ~~Personal details~~
Personal profile   Work experience

A *Personal details*

Name: Ulrike Helga Kramer
Address: 45 Cranley Gardens, London SW12 4QT
Email: ulrikeh_kramer@coolmail.net
1 _____

B _____

I am hard-working, and enjoy working in a team. I am also communicative and sociable, and have a lot of patience with people.
2 _____

C _____

2000–2004   doctorate, University of Manchester
1996–2000   degree in Chemistry, University of Berlin (first class)
3 _____

D _____

2008–present   Coldstream High School, London
4 _____

2004–2008   Fischer Chemical Industries
My responsibilities were organizing laboratory research. Tasks included coordinating research assistants and writing reports.

E _____
5 _____
I also play the violin and the guitar.

---

7 Match these new details with the correct gaps in the CV.
   a [2] Finally, I think I am a creative problem solver.
   b ☐ 1994–96 Gisele Friedrichs Hochschule, Hannover, Germany
   c ☐ Judo, cycling and photography.
   d ☐ Tasks include teaching Chemistry, exam preparation and student orientation.
   e ☐ Telephone: 07625 821965

8 Make notes for your own CV. Use the headings from Ulrike's CV.

9 Now write your own CV using your notes.

Now try the Self check on >> p.78.

How to say how you feel about things

4A

G -ed and -ing adjectives   V -ed and -ing adjectives   P -ed endings

A Grammar and vocabulary
-ed and -ing adjectives

1 Underline the correct adjectives in the news report.

Snake in the grass mystery
SMALLTOWN, WESTERN AUSTRALIA

When a four-metre-long snake appeared in a local park yesterday, neighbours were [1] terrified/terrifying and contacted the police.

Two friends who were walking through the park were [2] amazed/amazing to find the snake at the bottom of a tree. The police had to call in experts from a vet clinic to help them catch the animal. 'It's the most [3] excited/exciting thing that's happened this year,' said one man. 'I just feel [4] annoyed/annoying that I didn't actually see it myself!' 'I was [5] worried/worrying when I heard about it. I have two young children!' said another man.

Children however were [6] fascinated/fascinating by the animal, and wanted to touch it. 'Yes, I touched it!' said one child, 'And it isn't [7] disgusted/disgusting at all!'

The incident was also a little [8] embarrassed/embarrassing for the nearest zoo, which was unable at first to identify the snake. They have now confirmed it is not a dangerous animal. Officials were not very [9] interested/interesting in reporters' questions. 'No, it isn't one of ours. We only have smaller snakes,' they commented.

2 Complete the letter with these words.

amazing   annoyed   boring   excited   disgusting
embarrassing   satisfied   ~~worried~~

Dear Mum and Dad,

I got your letter yesterday. Please don't be so [1] _worried_ about me, because everything is fine here at Camp Windrush. Well, nearly everything. I have to say the food is really [2] _____! It's cold, and it doesn't taste very good. I really miss Mum's cooking! But the camp and location are absolutely [3] _____. We're in a forest, next to a lake, and there are mountains all around. There are so many things to do, too: boat trips, nature walks, tree climbing. A few of the other kids are a bit [4] _____. One boy was [5] _____ because he couldn't bring his computer games to camp! But most of them are fun. We all got really [6] _____ the other day because there was a fox under one of the camp buildings! The helpers are OK, although we have to work really hard for them. Yesterday, we had to do the same exercises three times before they were [7] _____. But then one of them got lost in the woods, and that was [8] _____ for him! Everyone just laughed!

See you soon,
Paul

3 Complete the sentences with adjectives from exercises 1 and 2.

1 I can't sleep! I'm so _excited_ about flying to Mexico on Sunday.
2 *Pacific Express*, a new thriller from Parapet Productions, looks absolutely _____ on the screen.
3 I get really _____ about all the TV adverts for children. I think the advertisers are just not responsible enough.
4 I always remember people's faces, but never remember their names. It's so _____!
5 The spiders in that nature programme looked absolutely _____! But I didn't realize they were so important to the environment.
6 Thomas wants to be an astronaut when he grows up. He's _____ by space, the universe and rocket technology.

B Pronunciation -ed endings

4 Write these words in the correct column.

~~stayed~~   ~~embarrassed~~   ~~waited~~   amazed
interested   annoyed   excited   relaxed   decided
fascinated   stopped

/d/	/t/	/ɪd/
stayed	embarrassed	waited

5 4A.1▶ Listen and repeat.

And you? Write about your own feelings.

1 I feel annoyed when _____.
2 I'm fascinated by _____.
3 I think it's embarrassing when people _____.
4 The most terrifying thing for me is _____.

How well can you say how you feel about things now?
Go back to the Student's Book >> p.37 and tick ✓ the line again.

How to talk about music

4B

G comparatives and superlatives   V music   P comparative -er

A Vocabulary music

1 Complete the factfile with these words.

concert   drummer   ~~group~~   guitarist   keyboards
musicians   singer   tracks   venues

FACTFILE
Classic '70s and '80s Rock

- [1] *Group*'s name: Queen
- Beginnings: early '70s performances at small [2] _____ in England
- Biggest [3] _____: Live Aid event, London 1985
- Most famous [4] _____: *Bohemian Rhapsody*; *We are the Champions*
- [5] _____ in the band:
  - Freddie Mercury [6] _____
  - John Deacon [7] _____
  - Roger Taylor [8] _____
  - Brian May [9] _____
- What do they sound like?
  Queen have inspired a lot of modern bands. If you like Mika, Muse or The Darkness, try listening to *Bohemian Rhapsody*!

B Grammar comparatives and superlatives

2 Complete the table with the comparative or superlative.

Spelling patterns in comparatives and superlatives			
Example	a long symphony — 1 hour	a longer symphony — 2 hours	the longest symphony — 3 hours
1	a big instrument	_____ instrument	the biggest instrument
2	noisy music	noisier music	_____ music
3	an expensive concert	_____ concert	the most expensive concert

3 Complete the sentences with the correct form of the adjective in brackets. Add any other necessary words.

1 This magazine says that Latin music is _livelier than_ Celtic music. (lively)
2 Sorry, but I think rock is much _____ _____ _____ Latin or Celtic music! (interesting)
3 For me, opera is _____ _____ _____ kind of music to listen to than pop music. (difficult)
4 Few styles of music are _____ _____ _____ heavy metal, in my opinion. (boring)
5 I still think U2 were _____ _____ group of the '90s. (great)
6 Studio albums have a _____ sound quality _____ live concerts. (good)
7 She says that *Without You* is _____ _____ song that she has ever heard. (sad)
8 In your opinion, what is _____ _____ _____ album that REM have recorded? (original)

C Pronunciation comparative -er

4 **4B.1▶** Listen and write *N* for normal adjectives, and *C* for comparative adjectives.

1 [N]   3 ☐   5 ☐   7 ☐   9 ☐   11 ☐
2 [C]   4 ☐   6 ☐   8 ☐   10 ☐   12 ☐

5 Listen again and repeat.

And you? Choose two kinds of music – one you like, and one you don't like. Write two reasons why your favourite kind is better.

I like _____, but I'm not keen on _____.

1 _____

2 _____

How well can you talk about music now?
Go back to the Student's Book >> p.39 and tick ✓ the line again.

23

How to compare and discuss preferences 4C

G comparing with *as*   V expressing likes and dislikes   P disagreeing politely

A Vocabulary expressing likes and dislikes

1 Match the two parts of the sentences.
1. [b] I absolutely adore
2. [ ] I don't like spending
3. [ ] I prefer
4. [ ] I'm not too keen
5. [ ] I can't stand slow
6. [ ] I don't mind

a lots of money in very expensive restaurants.
b ~~good Chinese food.~~
c on sweets and cakes.
d service in a restaurant.
e not to have potatoes with my meals.
f waiting for a table, if the restaurant is full.

2 Put the phrases in *italics* in the correct order to complete the conversation.

A How about eating out tonight?

B OK! What kind of food would you like?

A *I'd have Italian to not prefer* ¹ <u>I'd prefer not to have Italian</u> food again – we had pasta yesterday. What about Mexican? *meal just Mexican a good adore I* ² _____.

B Sorry, *on keen I'm too not* ³ _____ Mexican food. It's got cheese with everything, and they always serve it half-cold. *mind I food don't spicy* ⁴ _____ but *food getting like don't I* ⁵ _____ that isn't warm. How about Thai food?

A Thai? Yes, I love that! I really think Thai dishes *world the the best are in* ⁶ _____! How about that new restaurant on Burton Street?

B I think that one is really busy. *go to I'd prefer to* ⁷ _____ one that we know already.

A OK, let's go to the Phuket Palace then. I'll phone first, because *waiting stand can't I* ⁸ _____ in a queue either!

B Grammar comparing with *as*

3 Complete the sentences. Use the chart to help you.

THE GOOD TABLE GUIDE: Restaurant ratings

*** excellent
** satisfactory
* poor

	OASIS	Nanjing	EL DORADO
Value for money	*	**	***
Quality of the food	*	***	**
Capacity (number of seats)	**	**	***
Service	**	**	*
Takeaway service	***	**	**
Hygiene	*	**	**
Parking	***	*	*
Opening hours	**	*	***

1 The service at *Oasis* is as quick as in _____.
2 They don't have as much parking at *El Dorado* as at _____.
3 *Oasis* has seats for as many people as _____.
4 The food at *Nanjing* isn't as good value as at _____.
5 The takeaway service at *El Dorado* isn't as quick as at _____.

4 Make sentences about the restaurants in exercise 3. Use *(not) as ... as* and the words provided.
1 food / El Dorado / good / Nanjing
   <u>The food at El Dorado isn't as good as at Nanjing</u>.
2 Nanjing / clean / El Dorado
   _____.
3 takeaway service / El Dorado / quick / Nanjing
   _____.
4 Oasis / open / long / El Dorado
   _____.
5 value for money at Oasis / good / the other restaurants
   _____.

C Pronunciation disagreeing politely

5 4C.1▶ Listen to the suggestions and the reactions. Write *A* for an agreement, *D* for a disagreement.
1 [A] 2 [ ] 3 [ ] 4 [ ] 5 [ ] 6 [ ]

6 Listen again and repeat the reactions. Pay attention to the tone of voice.

How well can you compare and discuss preferences now?
Go back to the Student's Book >> p.41 and tick ✓ the line again.

24

How to explain what a film is about

4D

G defining relative clauses   V films

A Vocabulary films

1 Match the parts of the words to make different types of film.

1	f	act	-ance	a
2	☐	com	-tasy	b
3	☐	dra	-edy	c
4	☐	fan	-ical	d
5	☐	mus	-ma	e
6	☐	rom	-ion	f

2 Write an example for each of the film types in exercise 1.

1 _____
2 _____
3 _____
4 _____
5 _____
6 _____

3 Match the film descriptions with the definitions a–j.
1 [d] interesting, entertaining conversation
2 ☐ good-looking people
3 ☐ lots of different kinds of feelings
4 ☐ with interesting events, easy to follow
5 ☐ somebody that the main character finds attractive
6 ☐ how people get on with each other
7 ☐ martial arts or wars, for example
8 ☐ lots of different things happening
9 ☐ when events move very fast
10 ☐ the feeling you have when you're not sure what will happen

a action
b attractive men/women
c a good story
d ~~great dialogue~~
e emotion
f excitement
g fighting
h a love interest
i relationships
j speed

B Grammar defining relative clauses

4 Underline the correct pronouns.

The director ¹ who / which brought us the hit comedy *Life of Irmengard*, Jennifer Neufeld, has worked with actor Gary Fields to bring us her new film *Plastic Explosive*.

This is a social drama ² who / which tells the story of a group of women ³ who / which decide that rubbish is killing the Earth, and that it's time to go back to the basics: a life with much less plastic. The local shop owners ⁴ who / which accept their ideas gradually become more successful, and slowly their group becomes more important. But big supermarkets ⁵ who / which are against the idea start causing problems. There are also people in their own families ⁶ who / which don't want to change, and the film's dialogue is full of arguments.

At this point, a 'green millionaire' (Gary Fields) joins the battle. He creates the 'Plastic Explosive' website, ⁷ who / which has a million visits a week. Plastechs, the company ⁸ who / which produces 60% of the country's plastic bags, fires 500 workers. What will happen when the women meet the workers on TV? And will they really succeed in finding a replacement for plastic?

5 Complete the sentences with *who, which, that*, or nothing if you think it's possible to leave out the relative pronoun.

1 He's the man _who_ the police were following.
2 It was a computer virus _____ he sold to criminals _____ caused all the problems.
3 It was these criminals _____ used it to get government information.
4 The government had to change the energy programme _____ it had planned.
5 This is the journalist _____ discovered the story.
6 The police received a letter _____ identified the journalist as a spy.
7 His body was found in a car _____ he had rented for a holiday.
8 It was the journalist's boss _____ printed the whole story.

And you? Which things are important for you in a good film? Describe one film from your list in exercise 2. Use words from exercises 1 and 3.

Name of film: _____
What I enjoyed about the film: _____

How well can you explain what a film is about now?
Go back to the Student's Book >> p.43 and tick ✓ the line again.

Unit 4 Skills Practice

A Read a concert review

1 Read the text quickly and tick ✓ the best title.
   a ☐ Boring concert
   b ☐ Incredible concert
   c ☐ Wet concert

1 **The Skitsoid Kids** are on tour at the moment, to promote their new album *Slave Trade*. The 20-concert tour has gone well so far, with big crowds at most venues, and good weather as well. That's probably why last night's concert, number 17 of the tour, which was held in the Fanfield football stadium, was so disappointing. In terrible weather, their good luck turned into bad.

2 There were certainly a lot of great things about the concert. First of all, the audience of about 30,000 cheering fans who sang along to the songs. Most of them were in seats, so the two large video screens on each side of the stage were really helpful for everyone to see the musicians. The ten songs in the first part of the concert included classics like *Hate your Love* and *Go Down*. Melvyn Twigg gave a powerful performance on the drums with *Binge Day*. Micky Welch, the new keyboard player, did well on both the rock songs and the slow ballads. Welch has a very promising future with the band.

3 The problems started in the second half of the concert. Something went wrong with the sound quality and the singers' voices got lost in the overpowering music. Three songs later, the audience began to get impatient, because they still couldn't hear the vocals. And then suddenly heavy rain started and the concert had to stop.

4 All in all, it was a very acceptable performance at the beginning, but a disastrous ending for the concert. The organizers have promised a repeat concert for next Spring. Let's hope the weather will be better!

2 Match the paragraph numbers with the topics.
   a ☐ positive aspects of the concert
   b ☐ final opinion and conclusion
   c ☐ negative aspects of the concert
   d ☐ the group, venue and general opinion

3 <u>Underline</u> the correct answer.
   1 The new tour has already/<u>nearly</u> finished.
   2 *Hate your Love* is a well-known/completely new song.
   3 Most of the audience were standing/sitting at the concert.
   4 It was easy/difficult to see the group.
   5 Melvyn Twigg is a drummer/guitarist.
   6 Later in the concert, the vocals were too loud/too quiet.
   7 The weather was good in the first/second part of the concert.
   8 The band will/won't play at Fanfield stadium again.

4 Look at these adjectives from the text. Write *P* for positive or *N* for negative.
   1 [N] disappointing   6 ☐ overpowering
   2 ☐ cheering   7 ☐ impatient
   3 ☐ disastrous   8 ☐ acceptable
   4 ☐ powerful   9 ☐ helpful
   5 ☐ promising

B Listen and understand opinions

5 4S.1▶ Listen to two people talking about the *Skitsoid Kids'* concert.
   Write *M* for Max or *V* for Vanessa.
   1 [M] enjoyed part of the concert.
   2 ☐ thinks *Hate your Love* is the band's best song.
   3 ☐ prefers the rock songs to the slow songs.
   4 ☐ wanted to hear the band's vocals.
   5 ☐ thinks rain is worse than cold at a concert.
   6 ☐ wants to go to the next concert.

6 Match the sentences 1–6 with the things that the words in **bold** are referring to.
   1 [d] So what was **it** like?
   2 ☐ **That**'s my favourite.
   3 ☐ I can't stand **them**.
   4 ☐ **That**'s really annoying.
   5 ☐ I didn't know **that**!
   6 ☐ **That**'s good news!

   a slow songs
   b another concert next Spring
   c second part of concert cancelled
   d ~~the concert~~
   e bad sound quality
   f *Hate your Love*

C Read a film review

7 Complete the film review with one of these phrases.
at last   the end   then
the rest of the film   the story begins

Flightplan is a thriller that tells the story of a mother's desperate hunt for her daughter. ¹_____ when Kyle Pratt (Jodie Foster) falls asleep on an aeroplane. When she wakes up again, her daughter has disappeared.

Ordinary parents in that kind of situation might never find their child again. But Kyle Pratt is no ordinary mother. She's an aviation engineer, whose husband has died in Berlin. She and her daughter Julia are flying back to the USA with his body when the film opens. But nobody remembers seeing the girl on the plane. Worst of all, nobody really believes Kyle's story. Kyle persuades Captain Rich to search for Julia, but without success.

²_____ Kyle starts searching by herself, but she causes problems, so the captain orders Carson – the security officer – to keep her under control. Kyle, however, knows every part of the plane, and quickly escapes from Carson.

³_____ after Kyle's escape focuses on her efforts to find Julia. Despite all the difficulties, she doesn't give up. And when ⁴_____ she locates the girl, she discovers a much bigger problem that affects the safety of all the passengers on the plane. But she can't tell anyone, because they won't believe her. She must take action herself, especially when she is left alone with Carson, who is actually a hijacker.

In ⁵_____, Kyle fights Carson, and against people who say she's crazy. Foster's performance is just amazing – she really captures Kyle's determination and intelligence. You really see the extreme emotions she goes through.

8 Put the events in the order they happened.
a [1] Kyle's husband dies
b ☐ Kyle finds her daughter
c ☐ Julia disappears
d ☐ Kyle fights Carson
e ☐ Captain Rich orders a search
f ☐ Kyle escapes from Carson
g ☐ Carson must control Kyle
h ☐ Kyle starts her own search for Julia

D Write a film description

9 Read the film review and match the paragraph numbers with the topics.
a [3] What happens in the film
b ☐ The main characters and their situation
c ☐ What we can learn from the film
d ☐ Film, title, setting, and context

1 *Ratatouille* is a fun cartoon film about a rat that becomes a chef in a Parisian restaurant. It takes you into a special world where humans and animals live and work together. ¹In the end, these unusual friends manage to run a successful restaurant.

2 The film stars Remy, the talented rat. He plays the part of assistant to Linguini, the kitchen boy. Linguini is tall, thin and clumsy. ²He always wears a chef's jacket and trousers, and a tall white hat. The restaurant has not had very many customers. But Remy has lots of fantastic ideas for cooking, and soon it becomes a popular place to eat.

3 Linguini and Remy have to fight Skinner the chef and a health inspector, too. I like the part where the arrogant food critic Anton Ego tries Remy's special dish, ratatouille. That's a kind of vegetable dish in tomato sauce. ³You can also make it with sausages or steak, if you prefer. Ego believes he has found the perfect restaurant. But of course no respectable restaurant can have rats. And when the food critic discovers that a rat prepared his food, he goes completely crazy!

4 After watching *Ratatouille*, you will never think about restaurants in the same way again. I'd recommend it to anyone who enjoys animated films, or good food. You might even learn to cook better yourself!

10 The film review is better without the sentences in red. Match them with these reasons.
a ☐ extra detail not needed in a brief description
b ☐ reveals the ending
c ☐ information not relevant

11 Think of a film you have seen. Make notes for four paragraphs about your film. Use the four topics in exercise 9.

12 Write a short description and review of the film. Use your notes from exercise 11.

Now try the Self check on >> p.79.

How to talk about countries and governments

G the or no article in names of institutions **V** politics **P** the

A Vocabulary politics

1 Add *a, e, i, o,* or *u* to the political words.
   1 a c**o**ns**e**rv**ati**v**e** programme
   2 a liberal d_m_cr_cy
   3 _l_ct__ns in the spring
   4 a n_t__n_l symbol
   5 a p_l_t_c_l party
   6 the pr_s_d_nt of the r_p_bl_c
   7 an eagle r_pr_s_nts strength
   8 s_c__l_st ideas
   9 a meeting of the __n_t_d N_t__ns

2 Match the questions with the answers a–g.
   1 [c] When do they have elections?
   2 [ ] What's the national symbol?
   3 [ ] Which political party is in government?
   4 [ ] Which political views do conservatives have?
   5 [ ] Where do people put their voting papers?
   6 [ ] Does a republic have a king or a president?
   7 [ ] Which institution does the colour blue represent?

   a The socialist party.
   b Right-wing views.
   c ~~Every four years.~~
   d In a ballot box.
   e An animal.
   f The United Nations.
   g A president.

B Grammar *the* or no article in names of institutions

3 Write *the* or nothing to complete the sentences.
   1 How many countries are there in _____ European Union?
   2 Who is _____ head of state in your country?
   3 _____ Queen Elizabeth will visit _____ New Zealand next month.
   4 The Olympic Games were organized by _____ government of China.
   5 _____ Prime Minister has a meeting next week at _____ United Nations.
   6 _____ Liberal Party lost the elections, and _____ government is now controlled by _____ Conservatives.
   7 Millions of people respected the work of _____ Princess Diana.
   8 _____ King Richard III of England had a very bad reputation.

4 Add *the* to the newspaper article where necessary. There are nine examples.

French President is arriving in UK on a state visit tomorrow. He will have discussions with Prime Minister on relations between France and UK. The President will also speak to Parliament and have a meeting with leader of Conservative Party. In the evening, he's visiting Buckingham Palace for a banquet dinner with Queen. The next day he will travel to USA to speak at United Nations in New York.

C Pronunciation *the*

5 **5A.1** Listen. How is *the* pronounced in these phrases? Write them in the correct column.

   the British   the Americans
   the UN   the president
   the elections   the age of democracy
   the government   the Austrian president
   the Irish flag   the Republic of South Africa

/ðə/	/ðɪ/
the British	the Americans

6 Listen again and repeat.

And you? Answer the questions about your country.

1 How many political parties are there?
   _____.

2 Do you vote in elections? How often?
   _____.

3 Do you have a royal family, a president or a prime minister?
   _____.

4 What's your national symbol?
   _____.

How well can you talk about countries and governments now?
Go back to the **Student's Book >> p.47** and tick ✓ the line again.

How to talk about rules and laws

G modals of obligation   V permission words

A Vocabulary permission words

1 Tick ✓ if the two sentences mean the same. Cross ✗ if they do not.

1 ☐ a Parking is prohibited here.
   b You aren't allowed to park here!
2 ☐ a It's forbidden to take photos inside.
   b Photographs are permitted inside.
3 ☐ a Driving without a seatbelt is not permitted.
   b You are only allowed to drive with a seatbelt.
4 ☐ a Passengers are forbidden to open the windows.
   b Passengers are allowed to open the windows.
5 ☐ a Visitors are not permitted to wear shoes.
   b It's forbidden for visitors to wear shoes.

2 Correct the sentences. Use exercise 1 to help you.

1 It's forbidden use motorbikes on this path.
   _____.
2 Children isn't allowed in this pub.
   _____.
3 Parking are only permitted here at the weekends.
   _____.
4 You aren't allowed take this medicine.
   _____.
5 Driving without a seatbelt is prohibiting.
   _____.

3 Rewrite the sentences using the correct form of the word in brackets.

1 Walking on the grass is not OK.
  You _aren't allowed to_ walk on the grass. (allowed)
2 It's not possible to talk to the driver.
  Passengers _____ _____ _____ talk to the driver. (forbid)
3 Smoking in the hospital is not an option.
  Smoking in the hospital _____ _____ (prohibit)
4 It's possible to wear trainers in the club.
  Trainers _____ _____ in the club. (permit)

B Grammar modals of obligation

4 Complete the table using these verbs.

must   ~~mustn't~~   have to   don't have to   can   can't

Don't do this	Do this	You choose
a mustn't	c	e
b	d	f

Look at verbs e and f. Which verb do we use in these situations?
1 It's OK to do this, if you want to. _____
2 It isn't an obligation to do this if you don't want to. _____

5 Underline the correct word to complete the Queen's Park neighbourhood rules.

1 You must / can take your rubbish out to the bins.
2 You must / can put notices on the noticeboard, if you want to.
3 You can / mustn't smoke in the building.
4 You don't have to / can't water the plants, because the caretaker will do it.
5 You can / must collect your own letters.
6 You mustn't / have to play loud music after 11 p.m.

How well can you talk about rules and laws now?
Go back to the Student's Book >> p.49 and tick ✓ the line again.

How to talk about stories in the news

G active or passive? **V** crime verbs **P** compound nouns

A Vocabulary crime verbs

1 Complete the table with these verbs. Which one is not a crime?

arrest   attack   hijack   kidnap   ~~rob~~   shoot   steal

Crime verb	Verb objects
1 rob	banks, shops, museums, people
2	money, jewels, TVs, cameras, watches, bags, cars, credit cards
3	birds, wild animals, dangerous animals, people
4	people on the street, a country, an army in a war, a castle, your enemies
5	criminals, suspects for a crime
6	buses, trains, planes, cars, taxis
7	important people, rich people's families

2 Match the two parts of the sentences.
1 [h] A Panjam aeroplane was
2 ☐ The US president has been
3 ☐ 20 boxes of perfume were
4 ☐ A policeman was shot by
5 ☐ A tiger escaped from the zoo and
6 ☐ A man robbed
7 ☐ Police have arrested the two drivers
8 ☐ Thieves have stolen six

a kidnapped at a political meeting.
b attacked two of the visitors.
c six customers at a cash machine.
d paintings from the Central Museum.
e who caused the fatal accident.
f stolen from a supermarket last night.
g two men during a bank robbery.
h ~~hijacked in Chicago this morning.~~

B Pronunciation compound nouns

3 Write the compound nouns in the column with the correct stress pattern.

~~plane crash~~   ~~cash machine~~   ~~petrol station~~   murder victim
baseball bat   taxi driver   bus stop   bank robber   car key

●●	●●●	●●●●
plane crash	cash machine	petrol station

4 **5C.1▶** Listen, check, and repeat.

C Grammar active or passive

5 Underline the correct words.

A gang of four men ¹attacked / were attacked a local bank this morning. Two of the men ²shot / were shot the bank's security guard. Luckily, he ³did not kill / was not killed. The robbers ⁴gave / were given the keys by the bank manager, and then ⁵stole / were stolen the contents of all the security boxes in the bank. The police ⁶called / were called by a nearby shopkeeper. Unfortunately they ⁷did not arrive / were not arrived in time. In their escape, the robbers ⁸kidnapped / were kidnapped a bank customer, but this man ⁹found / was found later, unhurt. Five banks ¹⁰have robbed / have been robbed in the city in the last three months.

6 Write out the headlines in full sentences. Use the present perfect active or passive.

50 KILLED IN TROPICAL STORM
1 50 people _have been killed in a tropical storm_.

PICASSO PAINTING FOUND IN BOOKSHOP
2 A _____.

TWO SURVIVORS IN PLANE CRASH
3 Two children _____ in the Amazon Jungle.

SIX RESTAURANTS CLOSED
4 Six _____ by police this week.

MORE POLITICIANS ARRESTED
5 Following new evidence, more _____ in London.

And you? Write your news. Make sentences with the present perfect active and passive.

1 In your country:

2 In your town:

3 At school / work:

4 At home:

How well can you talk about stories in the news now?
Go back to the Student's Book >> p.51 and tick ✓ the line again.

How to talk about past events

G past perfect **V** war and power **P** stress in two-syllable nouns and verbs

A Vocabulary war and power

1 Complete the table with these words.

~~army~~ attack (vb) battle confess enemy
evil fight (vb) power protect rebels
rebellion soldiers

War and power	
people	actions
army	
events	concepts

2 Complete the account of a popular revolution with words from exercise 1.

We had a revolution here in 1894, after a short civil war. The people in the south of the country were unhappy with the government and started a ¹ _rebellion_. The government sent 10,000 ²s_____ to march south from the capital city. When the ³a_____ arrived, they rested for 24 hours. The next day, the general ordered his men to ⁴a_____. A violent ⁵b_____ continued for five days, and on the sixth day, the ⁶r_____ killed the general, and travelled north to the national capital. They said the government was the people's ⁷e_____, they had to ⁸p_____ the rights of the people, and they would continue to ⁹f_____ the government until they had control. A week later, the people's revolution took ¹⁰p_____ over the country. Since then, our country has been a socialist republic.

B Grammar past perfect

3 Complete the conversation with the past perfect form of the verbs in brackets. Use the picture to help you.

Mrs Atkins We were burgled last week. When we came home, we discovered that the thieves ¹ _had got in_ (get in) through a window. They ² _____ (drink) some beer in the sitting room, too, although they ³ _____ (not touch) our wine. They left beer cans everywhere! And they ⁴ _____ (smoke) our cigarettes! They ⁵ _____ (steal) our computer, with all my work on it, but they ⁶ _____ (not take) the TV or the radio.

Police officer You said there was a message on the wall. What ⁷ _____ (the burglars/write)?

MA I couldn't read it.

PO And ⁸ _____ (they/find) your jewellery?

MA No, thankfully they ⁹ _____ (not). It was still in the safe on the wall.

PO And ¹⁰ _____ (they/break) anything in the room?

MA Yes, a window and a lamp.

PO Thank you very much, Mrs Atkins.

C Pronunciation stress in two-syllable nouns and verbs

4 Underline the stressed syllable in the words.

1 <u>bo</u>dy
2 attack
3 column
4 reason
5 return
6 begin
7 neighbour
8 repeat
9 appear
10 building
11 picture
12 survive

5 **5D.1** Listen, check, and repeat.

How well can you talk about past events now?
Go back to the Student's Book >> p.53 and tick ✓ the line again.   31

Unit 5 Skills Practice

A Read newspaper articles

1 Match the headlines with the articles.
   a ☐ Man saved by cow
   b ☐ Film director dies
   c ☐ Rebellion in Central Asia
   d ☐ Cancer drug discovered

1 Chinese scientists say they have discovered a drug which will help stop cancer of the skin. The news was announced at a meeting in Beijing on Friday. The Chinese press have called it 'a major achievement'. Western specialists said that the discovery would 'bring hope to millions of people', and that they look forward to the results of more practical tests.

2 Rebel soldiers have taken control of a provincial town in the Central Asian republic of Khakiristan. Their leaders say they have not been paid for six months. The local airport has been closed and the army has cut all road and rail access to the city. Press reports say that the Minister of Defence has been accused of corruption. The situation is tense, but they have not reported any victims.

3 The life of a 35-year-old Swiss man has been saved by a cow. The man fell 20 metres off a bridge, but landed on the stomach of a cow which was lying on the grass. Doctors say the man is very lucky to be alive and can probably leave hospital in 3–4 days. The cow has a stomach-ache and did not comment.

4 Ronnie Bagelburger, one of the most controversial film directors of the 1980s, has died in his home in Los Angeles. His biographer says that his first three films were prohibited in 15 different countries. Many people hated the violence in his films, but many others adored his particular style of cinema.

2 Match the reports with the sources a–f.
   1 ☑ d New cancer drug discovery
   2 ☐ Waiting for drug test results
   3 ☐ Soldiers six months without pay
   4 ☐ No victims in Khakiristan
   5 ☐ Swiss man very lucky
   6 ☐ Director's films were prohibited

   a Bagelburger's biographer
   b Rebel leaders
   c Doctors
   d ~~Chinese scientists~~
   e Western specialists
   f Local newspapers

3 Match the highlighted words with their definitions. Check the pronunciation in your dictionary.
   1 to say what you think about something (vb) _____
   2 the way into a place (n) _____
   3 describing something that makes people argue and disagree with each other (adj) _____
   4 told people something important (vb) _____
   5 behaviour or actions that are not honest or legal (n) _____

B Listen to a holiday story

4 **5S.1▶** Listen to a conversation and complete the text.

John went to ¹ *Italy* to work in a summer ² _____. All the people on the project lived in a ³ _____ and shared their personal ⁴ _____. They had to share the kitchen and ⁵ _____. John shared a room with ⁶ _____. As for work, they had to clear the village ⁷ _____ and repair fences. But they didn't work at ⁸ _____, because then it was time to relax.

5 Match the two parts of the questions to show interest in a conversation.
   1 ☑ c Was it easy   a did you have to do?
   2 ☐ Did you have   b the experience?
   3 ☐ Would you recommend   c ~~to get along together?~~
   4 ☐ What kind of work   d actually do there?
   5 ☐ What did you   e a good summer?

6 Listen again. Then check your answers in the audio script on ≫ p.92.

7 Translate these questions into your own language.

32

C Read and follow events

8 Read the text quickly, and decide if its purpose is to:
a ☐ inform   b ☐ explain   c ☐ entertain

1. Question: what connects these three things – a man with a story about an old grey coat; another man with a photograph of a painting of a dead king; and fishermen's reports that they had heard gunshots? Answer: these three things could help to solve the 120-year-old mystery of how King Ludwig II of Bavaria really died.

2. Ludwig II – often called Mad King Ludwig – was King of Bavaria in the 1880s. He was famous for building romantic castles, for spending a lot of money, and for being eccentric. One day in 1886, his body was discovered in a lake near Munich, together with the body of his psychiatrist. The traditional explanation was that Ludwig, who had emotional problems, drowned himself in the lake.

3. In 2007, however, new clues appeared which suggest a different interpretation of events. An old man from Munich remembers that as a child he had seen the king's grey coat with two bullet holes in the back. An art historian has a photograph of a painting of the dead king, which was done hours after the king's death, showing blood coming from the mouth. If the king had really drowned in the lake, there would not have been any blood. And two fishermen reported in 1886 that they had heard gunshots on the lake. All of these clues have created new public interest in the case.

4. So the mystery continues. Was the king murdered? If so, who killed him, and why? The truth will only be known if his body can be examined by scientists. But for that to happen, his family have to give permission, and no-one is sure if that will ever happen.

9 Read the text more carefully. Which paragraph:
a ☐ asks questions about the future of the case?
b ☐ describes the events leading up to the king's death?
c ☐ introduces the mystery?
d ☐ gives new evidence about the king's death?

10 Write *true* or *false*.
1. King Ludwig's grey coat has never been found. _____
2. Ludwig died alone. _____
3. The text gives three new pieces of evidence about the king's death. _____
4. The painting of the king was done just before he died. _____
5. People heard gunshots on the day he died. _____
6. Ludwig's body has already been examined. _____

D Write a narrative account

11 <u>Underline</u> the correct words in the holiday story.

1. Barry and Selma were terrified. Where was their ten-year-old son Sean, and what [1] happened / had happened to him? They [2] only arrived / had only arrived at their apartment two hours earlier, and already the holiday was a disaster.

2. Everything had started so well. The whole family – Barry, Selma, and their children Sean and Lily – had wanted a seaside holiday, so they'd rented an apartment at a quiet resort on the Costa Verde in Spain. The children had been really excited when they arrived, so they [3] all went / had all gone straight down to the beach.

3. While Sean and Lily [4] have played / were playing in the sea, Barry and Selma had talked about their holiday plans. After a swim, Sean had said he wanted to go fishing at the other end of the beach. His parents told him to come back before eight o'clock, but by 8.30, he still [5] didn't return / hadn't returned. They went to look for him, but nobody had seen the boy. Everyone [6] got / was getting very worried, and decided to go back to the apartment to call the police. Just as Barry was dialling the number they found a big surprise.

4. The surprise was Sean, asleep in his bedroom. The boy had misunderstood his parents' instructions to 'come back', and [7] went / had gone to the apartment by himself. He was tired after swimming, and had fallen asleep. He couldn't understand why everyone was so worried. But when the police arrived three minutes later, he [8] promised / had promised not to disappear again!

12 Match the paragraphs with the narrative strategies.
a ☐ save the surprise until the end
b ☐ start in the middle of the story
c ☐ go back to earlier events to explain how the situation happened
d ☐ interest the reader in what is going to happen next

13 Write a story called 'The day I lost _____'. You decide what you lost. Before you write, think about:
1 Your ideas
   Who is in your story?
   What happens, where and when?
2 Your accuracy
   Think about the tenses you use, and how to connect the paragraphs of your story.
   Start at a dramatic moment in the narrative.

Now try the Self check on >> p.80.

33

How to express strong feelings   6A

G *so* and *such*   V extreme adjectives   P high intonation

A   Vocabulary extreme adjectives

1 Complete the adjectives in the table with *a*, *e*, *i*, *o*, or *u*. Use the table headings 1–8 to help you.

1 very good	2 very bad
am*a*zing br_ll___nt f_nt_st_c w_nd_rf_l	_wf_l dr___df_l t_rr_bl_

3 very angry	4 very big	5 very frightened
f_r___s	_n_rm__s	t_rr_f___d

6 very surprising	7 very tired	8 very intelligent
_m_z_ng	_xh__st_d	br_ll__nt

2 Complete the sentences with words from exercise 1.

1 The trip was _terrible_ – it rained all day long.
2 A fire started and we found the doors locked. We were t_____.
3 The weather was great and the kids loved the place. We had a f_____ holiday!
4 When he heard the news, he was f_____. He shouted at everyone!
5 Her house is e_____: it's got 20 bedrooms!
6 After a 30-km walk, he was e_____.
7 I'd love to see the film again. It was a_____!
8 No, I wouldn't recommend that restaurant. The food was a_____.

B   Grammar *so* and *such*

3 Underline the correct answer.
1 It's so/<u>such</u> a wonderful day that I think we should all go for a picnic.
2 She feels so/such bad that she's going to the doctor's.
3 The crowd were so/such furious that they attacked the police.
4 The kids were so/such tired that they all slept for 12 hours.
5 They're so/such a fantastic group that I go to all their concerts.
6 She had so/such a brilliant idea that they gave her a prize.
7 It was so/such terrible weather that the schools were all closed.
8 He was so/such terrified that he couldn't move.

4 Correct the mistake in each sentence.
1 Don't listen to Terry! He's such idiot.
   Don't listen to Terry! He's such an idiot.
2 Why did Tina get such nervous? Maybe she was just tired.
   _____
3 They shouted at each other in the middle of the party. It was so embarrassing situation.
   _____
4 He sent me all these flowers to say sorry. It was a such nice surprise.
   _____
5 Well, you know Henry! Sometimes he says so stupid things.
   _____
6 I failed my driving test again! I so feel depressed.
   _____

C   Pronunciation high intonation

5 ▶6A.1 Listen to the speakers 1–6 and write whether each one is expressing positive or negative feeling.

positive	negative
2	1

6 Check your answers in the audio script on ▶▶p.92. Listen and repeat.

And you? Write about:
1 a brilliant book
2 a fantastic experience
3 the last time you felt exhausted
4 a time when you were terrified

How well can you express strong feelings now?
Go back to the Student's Book ▶▶ p.57 and tick ✓ the line again.

How to **tell and show interest in an anecdote** 6B

G infinitives and gerunds

A Grammar infinitives and gerunds

1 Underline the correct words.

After ¹leaving / to leave university, I went to work in Germany. I was hoping ²learning / to learn more of the language. I'd been there before, in the north, and enjoyed ³talking / to talk to people. This time, I'd decided ⁴visiting / to visit the south. I was very surprised ⁵finding / to find that I understood so little of the language. I don't mind ⁶making / to make an effort, but this sounded like a different language! I hadn't expected ⁷having / to have such difficulties. But things soon got much better, and I stopped ⁸worrying / to worry about ⁹making / to make so many mistakes.

2 Complete the text with the correct form of the verbs in brackets.

What's so wonderful about ¹ _seeing_ (see) celebrities? Do you enjoy ² _____ (stand) in a big crowd and ³ _____ (wait) for hours just to see a famous person? We once decided ⁴ _____ (go) to a film première. We knew the actors would be there, and we hoped ⁵ _____ (see) them in person. Well, you can imagine what happened. After ⁶ _____ (wait) for nearly three hours, we discovered they'd had problems with the flight, so it was too late for them ⁷ _____ (arrive) in time. Six months later, we were in Paris on holiday, and guess what? We were lucky enough ⁸ _____ (see) the same actors in a restaurant – they were relaxed, and really happy ⁹ _____ (give) us an autograph! That's so typical: when you don't expect anything ¹⁰ _____ (happen), you get the real surprises.

3 Match the sentence halves.
1 ☐ Mandy stopped to buy
2 ☐ After searching all day,
3 ☐ Remember to get some
4 ☐ Do you remember playing
5 ☐ I can't stop to talk because
6 ☐ I remember taking out my wallet
7 ☐ Please stop shouting,
8 ☐ I must remember to return

a those books to the library.
b the neighbours will hear you!
c with these toys when we were young?
d to pay for the meal.
e they finally stopped looking.
f a birthday present on the way to the party.
g I'll be late for my train.
h milk on the way home.

And you? Complete the sentences.

1 I don't usually enjoy _____
_____.

2 This year, I've finally decided _____
_____.

3 I haven't yet finished _____
_____.

4 Next weekend, I expect _____
_____.

5 When I'm older, I hope _____
_____.

How well can you tell and show interest in an anecdote now?
Go back to the Student's Book >> p.59 and tick ✓ the line again.

35

How to talk about people in your neighbourhood

6C

G pronouns in reported speech   V behaviour   P spelling and pronunciation *gh*

A Vocabulary behaviour

1 Complete the crossword.

Across

1 (adj) describes people who shout or talk loudly
4 (n) person who uses pressure to control other people
5 (vb) if you _____, you use a lot of bad language
8 (adj) the opposite of 'rude'
9 (adj) positive adjective from 'friend'

Down

1 (adj) describes people who ask a lot of questions about other people
2 (adj) describes children who are good, and who do what adults want them to
3 (adj) positive adjective from verb 'help'
6 (vb) physically attack each other
7 (adj) describes children who don't do what adults tell them to

B Grammar pronouns in reported speech

2 Who is speaking? Write *P* for policewoman or *T* for travellers.

1 I want to see your passports! *P*
2 We're tired. ____
3 I've found something in your bag. ____
4 You can't keep us here! ____
5 That isn't our bag. ____
6 I'm afraid you're in serious trouble. ____

3 Write what the interpreter says for each of the sentences above.

1 *She says she wants to see your passports*.
2 _____.
3 _____.
4 _____.
5 _____.
6 _____.

Mike and Sarah get into trouble.

C Spelling and pronunciation *gh*

4 Write the *gh* words below in the correct column. Be careful with the pronunciation!

~~caught~~   ~~enough~~   fight   night   daughter   naughty
rough   neighbour   eight   bought   high   laugh   cough

gh = /f/	*gh* = part of vowel sound
enough	caught

5 **6C.1▶** Listen and repeat.

And you? Write about your neighbourhood.

1 The area where I live is _____.
2 Most of the neighbours are _____.
3 We sometimes have to complain about _____
   _____.
4 I know one family who _____.
5 The best thing about my neighbourhood is _____
   _____.
6 Some of the parents are unhappy because _____
   _____.

How well can you talk about people in your neighbourhood now?
Go back to the Student's Book >> p.61 and tick ✓ the line again.

How to report what people said 6D

G tenses in reported speech   V say and tell   P 'd

A Vocabulary say and tell

1 Underline the correct verb.

A I saw Sharon with that man from upstairs. She ¹<u>says</u>/tells he's her cousin, but I don't think so!
B I ² said/told you they were together! She ³ said/told me he was her brother-in-law! So where were they?
A In the Italian restaurant in George Street. And they were having a real argument, too!
B ⁴ Say/Tell me more!
A She ⁵ said/told she was going to leave him. She ⁶ said/told she'd seen him with another woman.
B Did he ⁷ say/tell anything?
A He ⁸ said/told her it wasn't true. He ⁹ said/told he would never leave her.
B Oh, they all ¹⁰ say/tell that, don't they?
A Yes. Well, then she hit him!
B No!

2 Correct the sentences.
1 She told to me a funny story.
   She told me a funny story.
2 He said me that it was late.
   _____.
3 Ellen opened the door and told 'Good morning!'
   _____.
4 Can you say me the time?
   _____.
5 What did they tell to the police?
   _____.
6 She said him that she had to leave.
   _____.
7 Could you say me the way to the station?
   _____.
8 They said me to sit down.
   _____.

B Grammar tenses in reported speech

3 Write direct speech for sentences 1–5 in the text.

> **The scam of the crystal skulls**
> In the 1920s, a man called Mitchell-Hedges told the world ¹*he had found a very old skull made of crystal*. He said that ²*the skull came from a pyramid in Belize*, and that ³*it was more than 3,000 years old*. Twelve other crystal skulls were later found in Central America. Historians said that ⁴*they couldn't be real, because ancient people hadn't had enough technology to make them*. The skulls were tested, and experts said that ⁵*they had probably been made in Germany, after 1850*. But many people still believe the story of the crystal skulls.

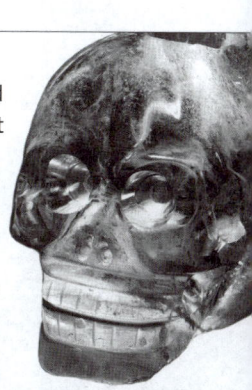

1 *'I have found a very old skull made of crystal'*.
2 _____.
3 _____.
4 _____.
5 _____.

4 Rewrite these claims about the Mitchell-Hedges skull in reported speech.
1 I found it in a pyramid in Belize.
2 I discovered it in 1927.
3 I'm sure it's at least 3,000 years old.
4 I believe it has magical powers.
5 I'm going to give it away.
6 Perhaps I'll give it to a Canadian museum.

1 *He said he'd found it in a pyramid in Belize*.
2 _____.
3 _____.
4 _____.
5 _____.
6 _____.

C Pronunciation 'd

5 Complete the rhyme with the words on the left.

didn't
~~have~~
made
needed
have
talked

She said he'd ¹ *have* to go
He said he ² _____ know.
She said she ³ _____ a break
He said he'd ⁴ _____ a mistake.
They said they'd ⁵ _____ enough
They said they'd ⁶ _____ to break up!

6 6D.1▶ Listen, check, and repeat.

How well can you report what people said now?
Go back to the Student's Book >> p.63 and tick ✓ the line again.   37

Unit 6 Skills Practice

A Read an opinion article

1 Read the text quickly and tick ✓ the best title.
   a ☐ Life without neighbours
   b ☐ Missing our neighbours
   c ☐ Model neighbours

¹_____ Who wants them? We all complain about them, but what would life be like without them?

²_____ There were seven floors, six flats per floor, 42 families all in the same building. The family downstairs were shouting and swearing all the time. The man upstairs practised his violin five days a week. The woman next door always complained about our dog, but when she had repairs in the flat, the builders and carpenters spent two weeks in the hallway. She said they would make her flat dirty! And when the lifts needed modernizing, half of the families at the community meeting said that the changes were unnecessary. We often wished for a quieter life, without so many people around.

³_____ We expected to have some peace and quiet. No more noisy neighbours, no more waiting for the lift, no more arguments at the community meetings. And then we noticed that the neighbours here are different. Nobody says hello. Nobody offers to look after the children for an hour, if there's an emergency. All we see are big cars, burglar alarms, and people who have no time to stop to chat.

⁴_____ The difficulties of living together don't seem so important now. In the block of flats, there was a sense of community. Whatever the problems, there were always other people around. We shared the same address and similar routines. Where we live now, it's certainly quieter, but it's also much less human.

2 Match the gaps in the text with these sentences.
   a ☐ Five years ago, we moved into a house.
   b ☐ In many ways, we miss our old neighbours.
   c ☐ We used to live in a block of flats.
   d ☐ Who needs neighbours?

3 Who are these sentences about? Read the text again to check.
   1 Who often used bad language?
      The family downstairs   .
   2 Who never say hello?
      _____.
   3 Who didn't like our dog?
      _____.
   4 Who played classical music all the time?
      _____.
   5 Who couldn't agree on modernizing the lifts?
      _____.
   6 Who misses their old neighbours?
      _____.

B Listen and understand conversations

4 6S.1▶ Listen to three conversations, A, B, and C, and match them with the topics.
   1 ☐ some lost luggage
   2 ☐ a lost car
   3 ☐ a lost camera

5 Match these expressions with conversation A, B, or C.
   1 ☐ Did you have to dig it out, then?
   2 ☐ Didn't you get them back later?
   3 ☐ Aha! But the thieves got in anyway.
   4 ☐ So what did you do?
   5 ☐ Hmm.
   6 ☐ What a shame!
   7 ☐ Uh-huh.
   8 ☐ And what was in the cases?

6 Match the expressions from exercise 5 with these functions. Write the numbers of the questions in the blanks.
   a Questions to show interest   _____
   b Expressing sympathy   _____
   c Adding details to show you understand _____
   d Making sounds to show you're listening _____

38

C Read a letter

7 Whose news? Read the letter and write *C* for Carrie, *N* for Nancy.
1. ☐ Matthew's accident
2. ☐ Jim's new job
3. ☐ Jim's grandmother
4. ☐ Irene's new flat

Dear Nancy,

Thanks for your letter. It was great to read all your news. I was sorry to hear about Matthew's accident. You said he had a broken leg, didn't you? Is he out of hospital now? Send him our best wishes for a quick recovery.

Well, we've got news for you, too – some good, some not so good. Jim's grandmother died last Sunday. We got a phone call at lunchtime, to say that she had fallen in the kitchen. Unfortunately, we didn't arrive in time to see her. I expect you remember that she'd been ill for some time. She was 92, and she'd had a fantastic life. We loved her a lot. We'll miss her a great deal.

The good news, however, is that Jim has now got a new job. Perhaps you remember him losing his job when the car factory closed? He went for a lot of interviews, but they all said he was too old. I mean, he's only 45! Not surprisingly, he was beginning to get a bit depressed. Thankfully, they phoned him yesterday to offer him a job at a local college, training mechanics. So he's really pleased.

Anyway, it was wonderful to hear that Irene's finally found a flat to buy. I'm so happy for her! It's so hard these days for young people to do that. What is it like? Wish her good luck from us.

That's all our news for today. It's time for me to pick up the children from school. Write soon!

Love,
Carrie.

---

8 Read these ways of making a letter similar to a conversation. Find two examples of each in Carrie's letter to Nancy.
1. expressing our feelings about other people
2. questions to show interest
3. expressing sympathy
4. writing about facts that the reader has already been told

D Write a letter to a friend

9 Complete the letter with these connecting words.

but ~~although~~ anyway by the way however

Dear Kay,

How are you these days? I hope your children are being good!

We're on holiday at the moment, ¹ *although* I have to go back to work next week. But it's great to have a change of routine. You would love this place: the walks, the little villages, the local food, the peace and quiet. ² _____ you would probably miss the nightlife! The nearest disco is 30 km away! ³ _____, there are lots of activities here to keep us busy.

⁴ _____, did you say something in your last letter about coming to visit us at home for a few days? There's plenty of room for the four of you. ⁵ _____, I don't think I told you that we have a new family member, a six-month-old dog! We've called him Dylan. Do the children have any pets? I'm sure they'd love this one!

Well, it's time for dinner. Don't forget to write and tell us when you're coming!

All the best,
Tom

---

10 Find references to these things in Tom's letter. Who knows about them? Write *K* for Kay, *T* for Tom, or *B* for both.
1. ☐ the children's behaviour
2. ☐ the holiday place
3. ☐ the nightlife
4. ☐ your last letter
5. ☐ room in the house
6. ☐ a new family member

11 What will Kay write in her reply to Tom? Match her notes a–d with the sections of her reply 1–4.
1. ☐ greeting
2. ☐ reply to Tom's news
3. ☐ my news
4. ☐ reply to Tom's questions

a Visit OK. Perhaps in May?
b Bought new car. More room for luggage!
c We're fine. Children OK, but Betsy ill.
d Lucky man! No holidays for us until summer.

12 What extra details could Kay add about items a–d in exercise 11? Make notes.
a *How about the first week of the month?*
b _____
c _____
d _____

13 Use your notes to write Kay's reply to Tom's letter.

Now try the Self check on >> p.81.

39

How to say how people look

7A

v looks and character; *look* and *look like*   P contrastive stress

A Vocabulary looks and character

1 Read the descriptions below and write the names of the people under the pictures. Use a dictionary to help you.

1 I'm Stella, and that's me in the middle. I'm ~~the youngest~~. I've got a small face, with short, straight hair. I used to have curly hair, but now I wear it straight. I'm confident and quite ambitious, too.

2 That's my sister Andrea, the one with the long face and long, wavy hair. She's a bit older than me. She's a bit shy, artistic too, and a really generous person.

3 There's my cousin Peter. He's very active. He's got a round face, and short, curly hair, and he's clean-shaven. He looks a bit like me, but he's much more nervous.

4 That one's my uncle Todd. He's a few years older than Cousin Peter. He's got a big, round face, and he's bald. He's an actor, and sometimes he plays unfriendly and aggressive people, but actually, he's very kind.

5 That's my aunt Martha. She's the oldest. She's kind of quiet and calm, but she's very imaginative. She's the one with the long, straight ginger hair and freckles.

6 The last one's my father, Richard. He's Aunt Martha's younger brother. He's got the same freckles, with a round face and a shaved head. He's just great – lively, outgoing and confident. He's a brilliant Dad!

2 Write the highlighted words from exercise 1 in the correct place in the table.

age	appearance	character
the youngest	small face	confident

3 Write phrases to describe the ages of the people in exercise 1.
1 Stella 13–19: _She's in her teens_.
2 Andrea, 15–16: _____.
3 Cousin Peter 27–29: _____.
4 Uncle Todd 30–39: _____.
5 father Richard 44–46: _____.
6 Aunt Martha 47–49: _____.

4 Complete the sentences with the correct adjective from exercise 1.
1 He speaks angrily, and sometimes he gets into fights. He's rather a_____.
2 She's so a_____ that she'll do *anything* in order to succeed.
3 Cathy's very creative. She's always making something, or writing i_____ stories.
4 No, Mark isn't at all shy. Actually, he's quite o_____.
5 G_____? My cousins? No! They don't share things with people and they only give small, cheap presents.
6 He's very moody and he isn't interested in meeting other people because he's so u_____.
7 Hannah's really a_____. She can paint, and she takes lovely photographs, too.
8 Mike would be a great sales person, because he's always very c_____ about his ability to succeed.

B Pronunciation contrastive stress

5 Predict and underline the stressed word in each answer.
1 Has he got long fair hair?   No, <u>short</u> fair hair.
2 Has he got short curly hair?   No, short dark hair.
3 Has she got big dark eyes?   No, small dark eyes.
4 Has she got small brown eyes?   No, small blue eyes.
5 Has he got a bald head?   No, a shaved head.

6 ▶7A.1 Listen and check. Repeat the answers.

And you? Answer the questions.

1 What does your best friend look like?
_____
2 What kind of person is your best friend?
_____
3 For each adjective, write the name of a person you know.
  a active _____   e generous _____
  b ambitious _____   f shy _____
  c artistic _____   g nervous _____
  d confident _____   h outgoing _____

How well can you say how people look now?
Go back to the Student's Book >> p.67 and tick ✓ the line again.

40

How to talk about fashion

G *wh-* clauses   V compound adjectives   P *t* at the end of a word

A Vocabulary compound adjectives

1 Match the two parts of the compound adjectives.
   1 [h] clean-   a off
   2 [ ] fashion-   b dressed
   3 [ ] good-   c mannered
   4 [ ] loose-   d fitting
   5 [ ] old-   e known
   6 [ ] well-   f looking
   7 [ ] well-   g conscious
   8 [ ] well-   h ~~shaven~~
   9 [ ] well-   i fashioned

2 Put the adjectives from exercise 1 into the correct column. Some can go in more than one column.

clothes	personal appearance

attitudes	social status

3 Complete the sentences with an adjective from exercise 2 which has the opposite meaning.
   1 Marco's family is poor, but his brother is very *well-off*.
   2 Personally, I think bald men are unattractive, although some women think they're quite _____.
   3 Even if customers are rude, receptionists must always be _____.
   4 Our mum is really quite modern – not like Dad, who is really _____.
   5 Tight trousers are not good for going running. You need _____ clothes for that.
   6 She doesn't care what clothes she wears. She's never been very _____.
   7 I think men with a beard just look untidy. I prefer _____ men, really.
   8 A I've never heard of this group! Who are they?
     B They're number one, Dad! And for people *my* age, they're very _____!

B Grammar *wh-* clauses

4 Complete the sentences with these words.
   what   when   where   who   why   how

   Ruth I don't understand ¹_____ we bought these dresses.
   Bill I don't care ²_____ the boss says: they'll never sell.
   R Can you tell me ³_____ to fasten this one?
   B I can't imagine ⁴_____ would want a dress like that!
   R Do you remember ⁵_____ I put the shop keys?
   B Do you know ⁶_____ the boss is coming in tomorrow morning? I think we're locked in!

5 Complete the second sentence so it has the same meaning as the first. Use a *wh-* clause.
   1 The jeans are very popular, but this isn't important for Bill.
     Bill doesn't care *who likes the jeans*.
   2 The blue dress is very cheap. This is difficult to understand.
     Ruth can't understand _____.
   3 Both shirts are great! It's not easy to choose.
     Bill can't decide _____.
   4 The trousers come from India, but this isn't important for Ruth.
     Ruth doesn't mind _____.

C Pronunciation *t* at the end of a word

6 **7B.1** Listen to the sentences and underline where you hear the *t*.
   1 I don't care what I wear.
   2 I can't imagine why you bought that.
   3 Your outfit looks lovely.
   4 Where did you get that dress?

7 Listen again and repeat.

And you? How fashion-conscious are you? Answer the questions.
1 Do you mind who designs your clothes?
2 Do you know which colours are in fashion this year?
3 Do you care where your clothes and shoes are made?

How well can you talk about fashion now?
Go back to the Student's Book >> p.69 and tick ✓ the line again.

How to talk about plans and intentions

7C

G future intentions   V body and exercise   P silent letters

A Vocabulary body and exercise

1 Complete the words in the boxes with *a, e, i, o,* or *u*.

1 parts of the body		
elbow	kn _ _	l_mb
th_mb	t _ _	

2 beauty treatments		
c_mb	h _ _ rc_t	m_ss_g_
sh_v_	st_ _m b_th	

3 exercises		
cl_mb_ng	gym	j_gg_ng
w_lk_ng	y_g_	

2 Complete the text using the correct form of words from exercise 1.

Male Icon Health Club

■ Some men get their exercise by ¹_____ round the shops, or ²_____ in the park, if they're feeling energetic. Maybe you prefer to exercise your limbs by ³_____ hills in the countryside at the weekend. But if you don't have time for that, come instead to the Male Icon Health Club. Here you can try anything from an intensive workout in our ⁴_____, to a relaxing ⁵_____ class. The Health Club will make sure your body is getting the kind of care it needs, from your head to your ⁶_____.

■ As a modern man, you look good because you style your hair with a ⁷_____, you ⁸_____ regularly, and get a ⁹_____ perhaps once a month. When you get tired, you might look after yourself by relaxing with a ¹⁰_____, or spending time in a ¹¹_____ _____. The Male Icon Health Club offers all these services – and more – for busy modern men like you.

B Grammar future intentions

3 What would you say in these situations? Tick ✓ a or b.
1 Someone invites you to a party, but you don't want to go because you're already busy.
   ☐ a *Sorry, I'll go to the cinema with Sonia.*
   ☐ b *Sorry, I'm going to the cinema with Sonia.*
2 You're with a friend, making preparations for a party. Your friend offers to get the drinks, and you want to get something too.
   ☐ a *OK, I'm going to get the food.*
   ☐ b *OK, I'll get the food.*
3 You're going to a party 90 km from home. Your friend would like you to stay at the house, but you'd prefer to make other plans.
   ☐ a *Thanks, but I'll probably stay overnight with a friend.*
   ☐ b *Thanks, but I'm staying overnight with a friend.*
4 You have two options for the holidays, but you're not sure which one to choose.
   ☐ a *Maybe I'll stay on the coast.*
   ☐ b *I'm going to stay on the coast.*

4 Complete the text with the most suitable future form. Sometimes more than one answer is possible.
   A They offered me the job last month! So ¹_____ (I/spend) a year in Canada!
   B Congratulations! When ²_____ (you/leave)?
   A Well, if the job starts in October, ³_____ (I/probably/need) to be there by mid-September. Of course, ⁴_____ (I/have to) arrange accommodation and things.
   B Hmm. And what exactly ⁵_____ (you/do) when you're there?
   A ⁶_____ (I/join) a laboratory team and ⁷_____ (we/do) research into people's memory.
   B So what ⁸_____ (you/do) between now and September?
   A Well, ⁹_____ (we/go) on holiday next month, and after that ¹⁰_____ (I/have to) begin all the preparations.

C Pronunciation silent letters

5 7C.1▶ Match the words in column A with words that rhyme in column B. Then listen and check.

A		B	
time 1 *climb*	sea 6 _____	calm	know
home 2 _____	fork 7 _____	half	walk
arm 3 _____	so 8 _____	knee	comb
drum 4 _____	laugh 9 _____	knife	thumb
life 5 _____		~~climb~~	

6 Circle the silent letters in column B.

How well can you talk about plans and intentions now?
Go back to the Student's Book >> p.71 and tick ✓ the line again.

How to express guesses

G modals of deduction *must, might, can't*   V adverbs for guessing

A Grammar modals of deduction *must, might, can't*

1 Match the two parts of the sentences. Use the picture to help you.

1 [b] He can't be a normal traveller
2 [ ] He might not be an artist
3 [ ] He must be going to a warm place
4 [ ] He might be a tourist
5 [ ] He might be bald
6 [ ] He must be a robber

BECAUSE

a his paints and brushes are unused.
b ~~he's got four passports.~~
c there's no shampoo or hairbrushes.
d he's got summer clothes.
e he's got a map.
f he's got a gun, a mask, and a lot of money.

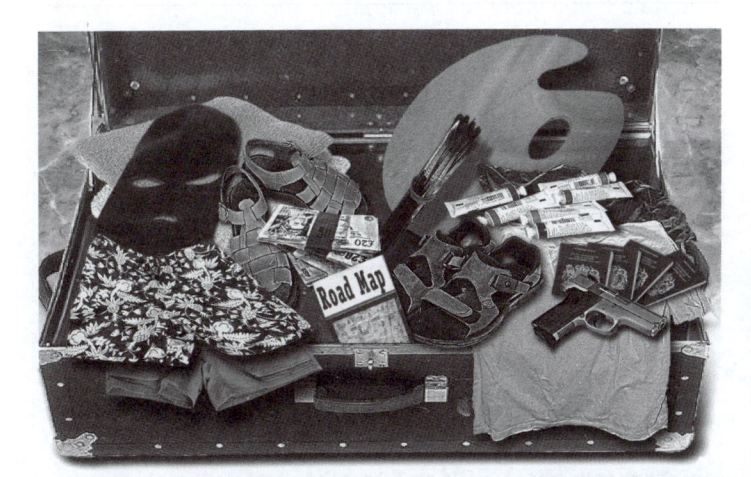

2 Complete the sentences with *might* or *can't*. Use the picture to help you.

1 She *might* be a mother,
  because there are photographs of two children.
2 She _____ be a doctor,
  because there are medical instruments.
3 She _____ be staying in a hotel,
  because I can't see any towels.
4 She _____ be staying very long,
  because she hasn't got many clothes.
5 She _____ be travelling to somewhere cold,
  because she's got warm clothes.
6 She _____ be going to Tokyo,
  because she's got a city map.
7 She _____ be walking very far,
  because she hasn't got any comfortable shoes.

B Vocabulary adverbs for guessing

3 Who is speaking here: the man from exercise 1, or the woman from exercise 2? Write M (man) or W (woman) in the box.

1 [ ] They won't search my suitcase. (probably)
2 [ ] They'll realize I'm a doctor. (perhaps)
3 [ ] I'll tell them I'm going to art classes. (maybe)
4 [ ] They'll want to know why I've got four passports. (probably)
5 [ ] I'll say someone else packed my suitcase. (perhaps)
6 [ ] I'll ask them to be careful with the equipment. (maybe)
7 [ ] They won't notice that my paints and brushes aren't used. (probably)
8 [ ] I'll ask them for directions to the nearest Metro stop. (perhaps)

4 Put the adverbs in the right place in the sentences in exercise 3.

Example:
1 They *probably* won't search my suitcase. (~~probably~~)

And you? What are your plans for the future?

1 Perhaps I'll _____.
2 I'll definitely _____.
3 Maybe I'll _____.
4 I'll probably _____.
5 I probably won't _____.
6 I'll think about _____.
7 I don't think I'll _____.

How well can you express guesses now?
Go back to the Student's Book >> p.73 and tick ✓ the line again.

43

Unit 7 Skills Practice

A Read for information

1. Before reading the text, think about what you would do if you went to Switzerland.

2. Read the first half of the text and tick ✓ what the writer is planning to do.
   - ☐ Go shopping
   - ☐ Visit the cities
   - ☐ Go skiing
   - ☐ Go walking and climbing
   - ☐ Go sailing
   - ☐ Go swimming
   - ☐ Try Swiss food
   - ☐ Buy Swiss chocolate

Travel Q & A

Q

My girlfriend and I are thinking of going on holiday in Switzerland this May, but we aren't sure what kind of things to take with us. We aren't really interested in skiing, but we'll probably mix a bit of city tourism with some walking in the mountains. Nothing very ambitious, but definitely a few days out to get some exercise. Also, my girlfriend is very good at sailing, so we'd really like to rent a boat for a few days on one of the lakes. But again, we don't know what kind of weather to expect, and sailing on a lake is not the same as sailing out on the open sea. Can you help?

A

That sounds like a very complete holiday that you're planning! Let's look at your ideas one by one.

↪ To begin with, the cities. You will probably need light clothes for the daytime: cotton shirts and tops, and comfortable trousers. You'll definitely need a good jersey or light jacket if you're going out at night, because it gets quite cool. You might want to take a set of formal clothes too, as the Swiss like to dress nicely to go out.

↪ Next, you say you want to take some day trips to the mountains. You'll obviously need some good walking shoes or boots, and a rain jacket, in case the weather is bad. Perhaps you should also take a survival kit, because mountain hiking can be dangerous, and there are accidents involving tourists every year.

↪ Finally, your sailing plans for the lakes. I think warm clothes for the evening would be the most important thing there. And don't forget a good pair of sunglasses, because the sun can be very bright when it's coming off the water.

3. Think about where the text is from and tick ✓ the possible source.
   - a ☐ a travel guide
   - b ☐ a travel magazine
   - c ☐ an online encyclopedia

4. Match the destinations with the recommendations for things to take. Some things are used more than once.

1 cities ☐b☐ ☐ ☐		a warm clothing
		b ~~light clothing~~
		c a rain jacket
2 the mountains ☐ ☐ ☐		d survival kit
		e sunglasses
		f boots
3 the lakes ☐ ☐		g formal clothes

B Listen to people's plans

5. **7S.1▶** Listen and match speakers A–D to their plans.
   1. ☐ Plans for the summer
   2. ☐ What to do after university
   3. ☐ Ideas about Christmas
   4. ☐ What to do after leaving school

6. Write the speaker who:
   1. ☐B wants to go to the beach.
   2. ☐ doesn't want to go to the beach.
   3. ☐ is going to go shopping on Friday.
   4. ☐ would like to work abroad.
   5. ☐ isn't going to work until September.
   6. ☐ prefers the weather in other countries.
   7. ☐ would like to spend time with two other families.
   8. ☐ would like to buy a car as soon as possible.

7. Listen again to A and B. How sure are they about their plans? Write VS for 'very sure', or NS for 'not sure'.

Speaker A
1. take a year off _____NS_____
2. go to Spain _____
3. look for a proper job _____
4. buy a car _____

Speaker B
5. find a Mediterranean beach _____
6. travel to Mexico _____
7. start a new job _____

C Read a magazine report

8 What are the main ideas in the report? Match the ideas a–e with paragraphs 1–5.
a ☐ The good things about the trip
b ☐ Suggestions for other people doing the trip
c ☐ Introduction from the magazine editor
d ☐ Preparing for the trip
e ☐ The difficulties of the trip

1 Last summer, the team at *Outdoor Europe Magazine* sent David Plant on a three-week walking trip across the Pyrenees, from the Atlantic to the Mediterranean. Now he reports back on his experience.

2 I had always wanted to go on a high mountain walk. There are some good long-distance walks in the UK, but there aren't any really high mountains. Before leaving, I checked my clothes, equipment, and the weather forecast. I also read a couple of books and looked at some photos and travel blogs on the Internet. This was fine, but you can't compare them with the real thing!

3 A lot of incredible things happened during the trip. Perhaps the best was the complete change from city life. While I was walking, there were no cars, no noise, no rush. The scenery was of course spectacular: valleys, mountain lakes, even a glacier, and there were plants and wildlife that you only see on TV documentaries. And I met so many interesting people along the way, from Europe, Canada, and Japan. The afternoon was always a good time of day, when I arrived at my accommodation and made new friends. They tell you where they've been; you tell them where you're going; you exchange stories and advice. It's just amazing!

4 But of course there are always problems. In this case, the weather. High mountains mean that the weather can change very quickly. We even had snowstorms in July! When your clothes get very wet, it isn't easy to dry them, so you're uncomfortable the next day. And climbing mountains is hard on your knees, too. And there's always the risk of slipping or falling on the paths, where not even a mobile phone can help you very much.

5 For me, however, the whole walk was a unique experience that I'll always remember. If I did the trip again, there's just one other thing I would do: lots of physical training before the walk!

9 Underline the correct option.
1 David *prepared* / didn't prepare for the trip.
2 He most enjoyed the peace and quiet / *meeting new people on the way*.
3 Bad weather meant that he *couldn't see the views* / was sometimes uncomfortable.
4 He had / *didn't have* a serious accident on the way.
5 On the whole, he feels he was / *wasn't* fit enough before doing the trip.

D Write a letter of application

10 Read David's advert for people to join a cycling expedition, and Martin Swift's reply. Which detail has Martin forgotten to include? Which paragraph would you put them in?

www.outdooreurope.net

- **Expedition**: cycle across Ireland, from Dublin to Dingle and back again
- **Dates**: August. Estimated time: 1 week
- **Distance**: about 700 km
- **Objectives**: exercise, tourism, and fun!
- **Apply in writing to**: David Plant, 4 Thornbury Way, Norwich, England

Please include: photo, personal description, interests, when you can travel in August, and reasons for going.

Dear David,

1 I am writing to apply for the cycling trip in Ireland. I saw your article in *Outdoor Europe Magazine,* and I thought it was a brilliant idea for an active break.

2 I am a 30-year-old Geography teacher. Last year I did a 10-day walk along the Welsh coast, which was fantastic. My hobbies include photography, mountain climbing, and of course cycling.

3 I would like to visit Ireland for several reasons. I've always wanted to go because my grandfather was Irish. And there are a few places I'd like to see for myself, such as Limerick.

4 I'm enclosing a photograph. It's not a problem for me to travel in August. I look forward to hearing from you.

Yours sincerely,
Martin Swift

11 Match paragraphs 1–4 with the information Martin gives.
a ☐ availability
b ☐ reasons for applying
c ☐ what he is applying for
d ☐ interests and experience

12 Now prepare to write your own reply to David's advertisement. First, make notes.
1 Where you saw the advertisement: _____
2 Personal description: _____
3 Interests: _____
4 Travel experience: _____
5 Reasons for going to Ireland: _____
6 When you're available to travel: _____

13 Write your own complete reply to David Plant. Use your notes and Martin's letter to help you.

Now try the Self check on ›› p.82.

How to talk on the phone

G phrasal verbs (2)   V phrasal verbs; telephone words and phrases

A Vocabulary phrasal verbs; telephone words and phrases

1 Match the two halves of the sentences.
1. [e] Sorry, I can't take your call. If you
2. [ ] I tried to call you this morning, but
3. [ ] There's a problem with the line.
4. [ ] I have to talk to you, so
5. [ ] I'll see if he's available.
6. [ ] Your brother wants to talk to you,
7. [ ] Could you just repeat that number, please?
8. [ ] Could you put me through
9. [ ] It's Ian again. I was leaving a message,

a to the sales department, please?
b but I got cut off.
c I couldn't get through.
d Could you hold on for a moment, please?
e ~~leave your name and number, I'll ring you back.~~
f I'm writing it down.
g I keep getting the engaged signal.
h please don't hang up!
i so I'll hand you over now.

2 Put the sentences in red in the correct order.
1 One moment, madam. I'm putting you through …
line please the you could hold

   Please could you hold the line _____?

2 Sorry, the line is still engaged.
can't through afraid I get I'm

   _____.

3 *Sorry, moment lines our are all busy the at.*
Please call back later.

   _____.

4 Sorry, we are not available at the moment. *message like a you if to would leave,* please speak after the tone.

   _____.

5 If you prefer to leave your name and number,
later back we you call will

   _____.

6 Can you give me that extension number again?
down to it need I write.

   _____.

7 Do you want to talk to Alec? *now over I'll you hand!*

   _____.

B Grammar phrasal verbs (2)

3 Underline the correct words. Sometimes both options are correct.
1 I'm afraid I can't come out, because my car's broken it down / broken down.
2 He isn't there? Do you think I could call him back / call back tomorrow morning?
3 If you wait a second, I'll put through / put you through to the manager.
4 Hang on / Hang you on a minute. I'll find a pen to write the number.
5 Alan was furious when I called! He hung up / hung him up before I could explain.
6 I don't think this phone is working. Every time I try to call, I get cut off / get it cut off.
7 Mike wants to say hello, so I'll hand over / hand you over to him now.
8 That was exhausting! It took 30 minutes to get through / get me through to customer services!

4 Complete the sentences with the correct form of these verbs. You may need to add a pronoun.

hang up   get away   hand over   hang on
~~get through~~   cut off

1 I haven't talked to the bank yet. The lines are busy, and I can't _get through_.
2 The police arrived in four minutes, but the attackers had already _____.
3 We were having a nice chat, until I suddenly got _____. The phone line just went dead.
4 Mandy isn't in the room. Can you _____ while she comes to the phone?
5 I'm sorry, but if you don't stop shouting at me, I'm going to _____.
6 Janet's just come home. I'll _____ to her for a quick chat.

How well can you talk on the phone now?
Go back to the Student's Book >> p.77 and tick ✓ the line again.

How to **talk about ability**

G ability *can, could, be able to, manage to*   P stress in words ending *-ity*

A Grammar ability *can, could, be able to, manage to*

1 Complete the sentences with the correct positive or negative form of *can*, *could*, or *manage to*.

1 A bear escaped from a zoo in Denmark yesterday, but police *managed to* catch it three hours later.
2 As a child, I _____ understand why we always had to go to bed so early.
3 **A** I'd like to be an actor.
   B _____ you sing or dance?
4 At school, my father _____ skate really well.
5 Did you _____ get the car repaired yesterday?
6 I lent her the money even though I knew she _____ pay it back.
7 Yes, I _____ understand some Japanese, so I'm happy to speak to him.
8 I tried three times, but I just _____ open the emails!

2 Complete the sentences with the correct form of *be able to*.

1 In the future, he *will be able to* play better.
2 Although the test was difficult, he _____ _____ pass it.
3 I've never _____ _____ understand philosophy!
4 The pilot _____ _____ fly the plane because of the storm.
5 To live in the countryside, you must _____ _____ drive.
6 With our new language course, you _____ _____ speak Dutch in three weeks' time!
7 I'm afraid John hasn't _____ _____ complete the test.
8 _____ you _____ _____ come to the meeting next week?

B Pronunciation stress in words ending *-ity*

3 Put these words into the correct column.

~~able~~ ~~curiosity~~ popularity possible reality
electric responsible quality opportunity quantity

adjective	noun
able	curiosity

4 Predict the word stress by underlining the correct part of the words in exercise 3.

5 **8B.1▶** Listen and repeat. Were you right?

And you? Write about your abilities.

1 I can _____, but I can't _____.
2 When I was younger, I could _____, but I couldn't _____.
3 I used to be able to _____.
4 I've never been able to _____.
5 I'd love to be able to _____.
6 I once managed to _____.
7 I don't often manage to _____.

I've never been able to skateboard!

How well can you talk about ability now?
Go back to the Student's Book >> p.79 and tick ✓ the line again.

How to report an interview

G reported questions

A Grammar reported questions

BRITISH 'MAFIOSO' SAYS HE'S INNOCENT

Naples police recently arrested an English businessman, Alan Smith, accused of Mafia activities. They have suggested he might be responsible for the murder of Giovanni Petrone, earlier this year. We talked to Mr Smith this afternoon, and this is what he said to our reporter.

1 Read the businessman's original questions, and correct the reporter's notes.

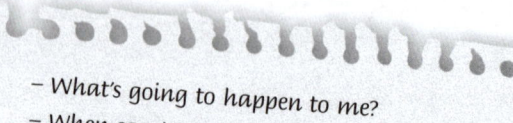

– What's going to happen to me?
– When can I see my lawyer?
– Where is the British Embassy?
– Why do people think I'm in the Mafia?
– When can I call my office?
– Are there any police who speak English?
– Can you pass this message to my wife?
– Will there be a trial?
– Do I have to pay for a lawyer?

1 He asked ~~if something was going to happen to him~~.
   what was going to happen to him.
2 He asked when he had seen his lawyer.
   _____.
3 He wanted to know if there was a British Embassy.
   _____.
4 He asked if people thought he was in the Mafia.
   _____.
5 He also asked why he couldn't call his office.
   _____.
6 He wanted to know where the English-speaking police were.
   _____.
7 He asked if we had passed a message to his wife.
   _____.
8 He asked when the trial would be.
   _____.
9 He wanted to know how much he had to pay for a lawyer.
   _____.

2 Read the events leading up to Alan Smith's arrest. Write the questions.

1 A man came up to me in the park and asked me what time it was.
   Excuse me! What time is it ?
2 Then he asked me if I collected butterflies.
   Do you collect butterflies ?
3 I said I did. Then I asked him why he was giving me a briefcase.
   _____ ?
4 He asked me if I wanted the briefcase.
   _____ ?
5 I asked him what was inside it.
   _____ ?
6 He asked me if I had received a message from the boss.
   _____ ?
7 I asked him what the boss had said.
   _____ ?
8 He asked me if I thought he was stupid!
   _____ ?

3 Write what the businessman tells his wife on the phone.

1 Which part of Britain are you from?
   The police asked me _where I was from in Britain_.
2 Have you ever been to Italy?
   They wanted to know _____.
3 What is your real name?
   They asked me _____.
4 Who did you talk to in the park?
   They wanted to know _____.
5 Why did that person give you a briefcase?
   They asked _____.
6 Do you have a Swiss bank account?
   They wanted to know _____.
7 Were you involved in the murder of Giovanni Petrone?
   They asked _____.
8 Are you a member of the Mafia?
   They asked me _____.

And you? Report a recent conversation you had with a friend.

1 He/She asked me _____.
2 Then I asked him/her _____.
3 He/She wanted to know _____.
4 So I also asked him/her _____.

How well can you report an interview now?
Go back to the Student's Book >> p.81 and tick ✓ the line again.

How to report a conversation

G reported imperatives and requests   V reporting verbs   P linking after *asked* and *told*

A Vocabulary reporting verbs

1 Underline the correct answers.
   1 'If you don't sign it, you'll be in trouble!'
     He invited/told us to sign the letter.
   2 'We aren't going to sign that!'
     We refused/promised to sign the letter.
   3 'It would be a good idea for you to sign this'.
     She invited/advised me to sign the letter.
   4 'Could you sign this, please?'
     She asked/warned me to sign the letter.
   5 'All right, I'll sign it.'
     I agreed/offered to sign the letter.
   6 'Shall we sign this, then?'
     We invited/offered to sign the letter.
   7 'Sign here, please!'
     He told/warned us where to sign the letter.
   8 'Don't worry, I'll sign in a minute.'
     I refused/promised to sign the letter.

2 Complete the speaker's reports with *to* or *me to*.
   1 The presenter invited _me to_ say a few words.
   2 I agreed _____ speak for a moment.
   3 After 20 minutes, she invited _____ stop speaking.
   4 I refused _____ stop speaking, because I hadn't finished.
   5 I promised _____ finish speaking in five minutes.
   6 She advised _____ remember the time.

B Grammar reported imperatives and requests

3 What did the speaker and the presenter actually **say**? Write the direct speech for the sentences in exercise 2.
   1 _Would you like to say a few words_ ?
   2 _Yes, all right. I'll speak for a moment_ .
   3 _____ ?
   4 _____ .
   5 _____ .
   6 _____ .

4 Read the rest of the conversation between the impatient presenter and the boring speaker.

   Presenter ¹*I'll let you speak again* later if you like. But now ²*you really must stop* immediately!

   Speaker   ³*OK, OK, I'll just finish this sentence.*

   Presenter You've talked for over two hours! ⁴*Leave the room this minute, or I'll call security!*

   Speaker   ⁵*I'm not going to listen* to this nonsense! I'm going home.

5 Now report the parts in red. Use the correct form of these verbs.
   tell   refuse   agree   offer   warn
   1 _She offered to let him speak again_ .
   2 She _____ .
   3 He _____ .
   4 She _____ .
   5 He _____ .

C Pronunciation linking after *asked* and *told*

6 Complete the rhyme with *me* or *him*.

   He asked ¹ _me_ not to pack.
   I told ² _____ not to wait.
   He asked ³ _____ to call ⁴ _____ back.
   I told ⁵ _____ it was just too late.
   He told ⁶ _____ I'd be sorry.
   I told ⁷ _____ not to worry.
   And left ⁸ _____ by the gate.

7 **8D.1** ▶ Listen and check.

8 Listen again and repeat the rhyme.

How well can you report a conversation now?
Go back to the Student's Book >> p.83 and tick ✓ the line again.   49

Unit 8 Skills Practice

A Read an anecdote

1 Read the story and number the pictures in order.

a ☐

b ☐

c ☐

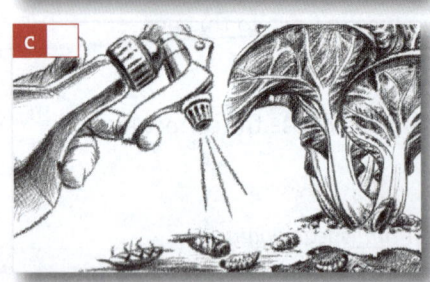

Have I told you the story of my girlfriend in Thailand? It's a lovely story of how well people manage to communicate, even if they don't speak the same language.

Well, my girlfriend and I were living in a rented flat, which had a tiny garden outside. And in the garden we planted some vegetables. The only problem was the insects. There were hundreds of them, and the plants weren't growing properly. Julie, my girlfriend, had only been in Thailand about a month, so she didn't speak the language. You can probably imagine how she managed. She communicated by pointing at things in shops, and then counting on her fingers, to show how many she wanted. And smiling a lot, of course. She was very good at that.

Anyway, going back to the problem of the insects, they were eating all the vegetables, so Julie really had to do something to stop them. She's a very practical person, so she put some of the insects in a plastic bag, and went down to one of the shops near the market. In the shop, she showed the owner the insects in the bag, and then made a sign of cutting her throat, to show that she wanted to kill them. The man didn't understand at first, but then his wife made the same sign, and laughed. Then they all laughed, and they sold Julie some insecticide, which worked perfectly. And after that, each time she passed the shop, the owners would wave to her with a big smile, and make that sign of cutting throats!

2 Answer the questions.
 1 Think about the main purpose of the story. Tick ✓ whether you think it is to:
  a ☐ inform   b ☐ explain   c ☐ entertain
 2 The message of the story is to show
  a ☐ how important it is to learn a foreign language.
  b ☐ that you can communicate well without words.
  c ☐ how cultural misunderstandings happen.

3 Read the story again. Write *True* or *False*.
 1 They bought the flat with the tiny garden.   *False*
 2 Julie could read and write Thai quite well.   _____
 3 Julie took a plastic bag down to the shop.   _____
 4 Julie knew the Thai word for 'kill'.   _____
 5 The shop owners understood what she meant straight away.   _____
 6 Julie got exactly what she needed from the shop.   _____

B Listen to an anecdote

4 8S.1▶ Listen to a story and put the events in order.
 a ☐6☐ Saskia ran out of the shop.
 b ☐ A man bought two dresses.
 c ☐ Saskia went to find a bigger dress.
 d ☐ The man returned to change one of the dresses.
 e ☐ The man drove off in a van.
 f ☐ The shop computer and cash till disappeared.

5 Read the sentences and predict who says them. Write *S* for speaker, or *L* for listener. Then check your answers in the audio script on ≫ p.93.
 1 ☐S☐ The most incredible thing happened to her last week.
 2 ☐ What was that?
 3 ☐ Maybe he was in a hurry.
 4 ☐ No, no! It's all true.
 5 ☐ When she came out, he was gone.
 6 ☐ You're joking!

50

C Read for the main points

6 Read the first sentence only of each paragraph of the text. Match the paragraph numbers with these topics.
a ☐ Things the tourists felt negative about
b ☐ Introduction to the report – who's writing it, and what it's about
c ☐ Things the tourists liked

What do tourists think?

1   A national magazine recently decided to conduct a survey on tourism. They received many letters from local people on the subject. But first they talked to tourists in the street. They interviewed men and women from different countries, to find out what they thought.

2   Many of the positive answers were fairly predictable, while others were more surprising. 90% of those interviewed said what they most enjoyed was the weather. Another high percentage – 84% – were very positive about the food in the local restaurants. 75% were very enthusiastic about the local festivals, and said that it was wonderful to see how people had kept up their traditions even into the 21st century. Many said this had not happened in their own countries. 60% commented that local people were very helpful and patient with foreign visitors. Interviewees praised the schoolchildren in particular, who were very good, they said, at dealing with communication problems politely.

3   Some of the answers, on the other hand, were not so positive. 70% of the interviewees complained about prices, and said that these had become more expensive in recent years. 50% also complained that many souvenir shops had the same prices, which wasn't very competitive.

7 What were the tourists' impressions? Write *P* for positive or *N* for negative.
1 ☐P local festivals
2 ☐ food
3 ☐ prices in general
4 ☐ relations with local people
5 ☐ souvenir shop prices
6 ☐ the weather

8 Match the highlighted words with these definitions. Check the pronunciation in your dictionary.
1 as good as, or better than, a similar thing (adj) _____
2 always behaving in a similar way (adj) _____
3 a number or amount, measured out of a hundred (n) _____
4 behaving in a well-mannered way (adv) _____
5 showing great excitement (adj) _____

D Write a survey report

9 Complete the introduction to another report on tourism with these expressions.
however   if   in order to   so   this

Last time, we discussed tourists' opinions on the places they visit. [1]_____ give a balanced view, [2]_____, we then decided to look at the opposite side of the story: local people's opinions of tourists. [3]_____ we interviewed 50 men and women, and asked them [4]_____ they were happy with the situation. [5]_____ is what we found.

10 Underline the correct quantity expression to express the survey results.
1 The most / **Most of the** people we talked to thought tourism was a good thing.
2 The half / Half of the people thought that tourists spend a lot of money.
3 None / No of the survey group thought tourism raised crime in the town.
4 People generally think / thinks that tourists try hard to communicate.
5 The 40% / 40% of the group felt that tourists make prices higher.
6 Most / Almost all of the people thought tourist buses cause traffic problems.

11 Underline the correct words to complete the conclusion to the survey, using the results in exercise 10.

On the whole, we could say that [1]most/few people are happy with the contact they have with visitors. Opinions were [2]divided/the same on several points, such as higher prices and traffic problems, but the overall impressions were quite [3]positive/negative.

12 Use the paragraph plan below to make notes on the information in exercises 9–11.
Introduction: _____
Question: _____
Results: _____
_____
_____
Conclusion: _____

13 Use the paragraph plan and your own ideas to write about opinions on tourism in your own area.

Now try the Self check on >> p.83.

51

How to make small talk

G tag questions   V weather   P tag questions

A Vocabulary weather

1 Complete the word puzzle. Find the missing word at number 9.

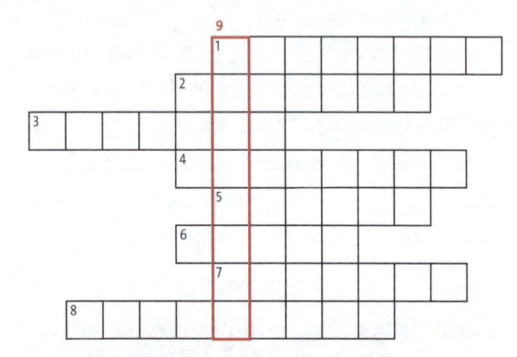

1 Very, very cold
2 Very, very hot
3 Short periods of rain
4 Unusually hot weather
5 These look very dark when they are full of rain
6 Very strong winds
7 Very, very wet
8 A violent electrical light in the sky when there are storms

2 Complete the sentences with these words.

~~boiling~~ floods freezing gale lightning
pouring shower snowing windy

1 The worst thing about a Mediterranean summer is the _boiling_ hot weather!
2 The worst thing about a northern winter is the _____ cold weather!
3 I love the silence when it's _____ in winter.
4 I don't feel like going out when it's _____ with rain, not even with an umbrella.
5 Heavy rain has caused serious _____ in our neighbourhood recently.
6 The big tree in the park burned down when it was hit by _____.
7 You won't need an umbrella! This is just a ten-minute _____.
8 Be careful if you go out. It isn't just _____, it's blowing a real _____ out there!

B Grammar tag questions

3 Write the correct tag questions to complete Patrick and Brian's conversation.

Patrick Excuse me, have you been waiting long?
Brian Yes, about 15 minutes. The bus is taking longer than usual today, ¹_____?
P Yes, it is. You don't know the time, ²_____?
B It's 9.20. You aren't in a hurry, ³_____?
P Yes, I am. I've got an appointment at the bank. I want a loan for a new car.
B You need a lot of money for that, ⁴_____? Cars are expensive these days, ⁵_____? And interest rates aren't very good either, ⁶_____?
P Are you looking for a loan too?
B No, but you're Patrick Henderson, ⁷_____? I recognize you from the photo on your loan application form. I'm Brian Talbot, the bank manager you're going to see!

4 Match the statements and tags to make a conversation.

1 [b] It's strange weather today,
2 ☐ Those clouds don't look very good,
3 ☐ It looks like rain over there,
4 ☐ The rain never lasts long though,
5 ☐ It'll rain later,
6 ☐ It isn't very cold,
7 ☐ You've got a real passion for weather,
8 ☐ You haven't noticed I'm trying to read,

a is it?
b ~~isn't it?~~
c do they?
d have you?
e haven't you?
f does it?
g doesn't it?
h won't it?

5 9A.1▶ Listen and check your answers to exercise 4.

C Pronunciation tag questions

6 9A.1▶ Which words in exercise 4 have the main stress? Listen again and repeat.

How well can you make small talk now?
Go back to the Student's Book >> p.87 and tick ✓ the line again.

How to talk about your future

G future perfect V parts of the body; attitude adverbs P stressed and unstressed words

A Vocabulary parts of the body; attitude adverbs

1 Underline the correct words.

1 I've had my hair/the hairs cut. What do you think?
2 I want to grow my fingernails/finger's nails.
3 She's got beautiful eyes, with lovely long eyebrows/eyelashes.
4 Many children learn to count by using the/their fingers.
5 My back hurts/It hurts me the back.
6 Have you got anything for a pain in the head/a headache?

2 Complete the predictions using the adverbs below and the words in brackets in a suitable future tense.

hopefully   probably   unfortunately   definitely

1 I'd like to be able to go to the USA next year. (visit)
   Hopefully, I'll be able to visit the USA next year.
2 He wants to start university, but that's not going to happen.
   He _____. (not go)
3 Duffy is playing a concert here in the summer and my sister works in the ticket office.
   I _____. (see)
4 It's winter and temperatures are falling fast.
   It _____. (snow)
5 Our company has agreed to pay us more in January.
   We _____. (get/pay rise)
6 We'd like a new car, but we haven't got enough money.
   _____, we _____. (not buy)
7 He adores her and she adores him.
   They _____. (get married)
8 We'd love the Green Party to win the elections, but they're a minority.
   They _____. (not win)

B Grammar future perfect

3 Make future perfect sentences using these verbs. Use the Life Plans chart to help you.

plant   repay   wash   buy   repair   ~~answer~~   build   write

LIFE PLANS	
2050	no mortgage to pay
40TH BIRTHDAY	my novel
CHRISTMAS	house extension
SUMMER	better kitchen
MARCH	new trees in garden
WEEKEND	broken bike
AFTERNOON	dirty car
12.00	emails in inbox

1 By twelve o'clock, I *'ll have answered* those emails.
2 By this afternoon, I _____ the car.
3 By the weekend, I _____ my bike.
4 By March, we _____ trees in the garden.
5 By the summer, we _____ a new kitchen.
6 By Christmas, we _____ the house extension.
7 By the time I'm 40, I _____ a novel.
8 By the year 2050 we _____ the mortgage.

C Pronunciation stressed and unstressed words

4 Predict and underline the stressed words.
1 My sister will have left school.
2 My father will have stopped working.
3 I'll have finished my degree.
4 My sister won't have got married.
5 My brother won't have left home.
6 I won't have bought a flat.

5 **9B.1▶** Listen and repeat the sentences.

And you? Complete the sentences with a suitable future form.

1 By 2020, I'll _____.
2 Hopefully, I'll _____.
3 I definitely won't _____.
4 Next week, I'll probably _____.
5 By the time I retire, I'll _____.

How well can you talk about your future now?
Go back to the Student's Book >> p.89 and tick ✓ the line again.

How to give advice

G 1st conditional; *if* clauses   **V** direction of movement

A Vocabulary direction of movement

1 Complete the sentences with these words.

along   backwards   downhill   downwards
forwards   inside   outside   towards
~~uphill~~   upwards

1 The man is looking _uphill_ and the snowball is rolling _____.
2 A is cycling _____, but B is cycling _____.
3 C is swimming _____, while D is swimming _____.
4 E is going _____, but F is coming _____.
5 G is running _____ the street, and H is cycling _____ him.

2 <u>Underline</u> the correct word.
1 If your balloon escapes, it will probably fly upwards/towards.
2 When you want to park a car, you often need to drive it forwards/backwards.
3 In ski competitions, the starting point is uphill/downhill and the finishing line is uphill/downhill.
4 If you get a promotion at work, you move upwards/downwards.
5 If you don't like the rain, go inside/uphill.
6 Fish always swim forwards/backwards.
7 Can you take the rubbish inside/outside, please?
8 To get to the bank, walk along/towards this street and then turn left.

B Grammar 1st conditional; *if* clauses

3 Put the advice in red in order.

WALKING IN THE MOUNTAINS

1 If you think you're lost, *on position map your the check*.
   check your position on the map.
2 If you're walking for the whole day, *someone going which tell you're way*.
   _____
3 *new you buy some shoes should* if you don't have good walking boots.
   _____
4 *somewhere to dry for look keep*, if it starts raining.
   _____
5 *back immediately should you turn*, if there's a heavy storm.
   _____
6 *while rest a stop for and* if you get very tired.
   _____

4 What will happen if you don't follow the advice? Put the verbs in brackets in the correct tense.
1 If you _don't take_ (not take) a map, you _____ (get) lost.
2 Nobody _____ (look) for you if you _____ (not tell) people where you're going.
3 You _____ (have) sore feet if you _____ (not wear) the right kind of boots.
4 If you _____ (walk) in very wet clothes, you _____ (catch) a bad cold.
5 If a storm _____ (appear), it _____ (become) dangerous.
6 You _____ (fall) asleep if you _____ (rest) for too long.

And you? For each situation, write some advice for **A**, and a prediction for **P**.

1 If your computer crashes, **A** _turn it off and restart it_
   P _it will cost a lot of money to repair_
2 If you visit my home town, **A** _____
   P _____
3 If you want to be healthy, **A** _____
   P _____
4 If you want to learn my language, **A** _____
   P _____
5 If you don't know how to cook, **A** _____
   P _____

How well can you give advice now?
Go back to the Student's Book >> p.91 and tick ✓ the line again.

How to **talk about unreal situations**

G 2nd conditional V compound nouns P linking in questions

A Grammar 2nd conditional

1 Match the two parts of the sentences.

1 [c] If I did this more often,
2 [ ] If the children weren't playing,
3 [ ] My mother could help me
4 [ ] I wouldn't have to wash up
5 [ ] I would know what to do
6 [ ] This would be so much quicker
7 [ ] We wouldn't have much money
8 [ ] I could be watching the football

a I'd tell them to do the cleaning.
b if we had a dishwasher.
c ~~it wouldn't take me so long.~~
d if she was here.
e if I didn't have to do this.
f if they taught us these things at school.
g if we ate out more often.
h if we spent more on eating out.

2 Complete the second sentence so that it has the same meaning as the first.
1 Katie watches late-night TV, so she's always tired in the morning.
   If Katie didn't watch late-night TV, she wouldn't be tired in the morning.
2 She drives the kids to school, but she gets stressed in the traffic.
   If _____.
3 She doesn't go to the gym, so she doesn't feel fit.
   If _____.
4 She earns a lot of money, so she doesn't worry about the bills.
   If _____.
5 She doesn't have a pet, and she feels lonely.
   If _____.
6 She works from home, so she doesn't have to travel to the office every day.
   If _____.

B Vocabulary compound nouns

3 Put the words below into the correct columns to make more compound nouns. Use the keywords in the middle column to help you.

bell   club   medical   provider   ~~mobile~~   laptop
keyboard   text   room   ~~number~~   fiction   smoke

noun +	keyword	+ noun
car / public / 1 *mobile*	**phone**	book / call / 2 *number*
health / Internet / 3 ___	**service**	charge / 4 ___
address / phrase / 5 ___	**book**	fair / shop / 6 ___
computer / natural / 7 ___	**science**	lesson / teacher / 8 ___
desktop / personal / 9 ___	**computer**	graphics / programmer / 10 ___
burglar / fire / 11 ___	**alarm**	call / clock / 12 ___

C Pronunciation linking in questions

4 Underline the /dʒ/ sounds.
Where di<u>d y</u>ou go, why did you go?
Who did you see, what did you see?
Why did you not tell me?

How would you know, when would you know?
Who would you choose, which would you choose?
When would you let me go?

5 **9D.1▸** Listen and repeat.

How well can you talk about unreal situations now?
Go back to the Student's Book >> p.93 and tick ✓ the line again.

55

Unit 9 Skills Practice

A Read for general meaning

1 Read the charity advertisement quickly and decide the correct order of paragraphs A–C.

  1 ☐   2 ☐   3 ☐

2 Which paragraph
  ☐ gives more details?
  ☐ calls for action?
  ☐ presents the problem?

ORPHANS IN AFRICA
Can you help?

A Is there nothing we can do? Fortunately, there are solutions. Firstly, the right kind of medicine can keep parents alive for longer. Secondly, foster parents can take children into their homes until they are old enough to work. Thirdly, food and health care programmes can also be organized. But, like everything in life, all these things need money. If you worry about orphans, you can help us to help them. £20 a month will help one of these children survive. Call us at **Orfancare**, on **0112-687-4933** or visit our website **www.orfancare.org**.

B Why not think about that for a minute? If these children have no parents, they probably won't go to school. What's more, if they lose their homes, they'll live in groups in the streets. Moreover, if they want to eat, they'll probably have to look for food in the rubbish. In addition, children like these are often the victims of violence and crime, so they'll sometimes become child soldiers in local wars. On top of that, many older children have to look after three or four younger children, with no help from parents or grandparents.

C Do you ever stop to think about the future? Maybe you worry about a job, or the kind of car you'd like to buy. Maybe you worry about the exams you need to pass, or who your children are with at the moment. If you lived in Africa, maybe you'd worry about orphans: the 40 million or more children who have lost one or both parents because of war, AIDS, or other diseases.

3 Read the advertisement more carefully, and write *true*, *false* or *doesn't say*.
  1 40 million African children have lost their parents in a war. _____
  2 Most African children are unable to attend school. _____
  3 There's a chance that orphaned children will become child soldiers. _____
  4 Many African children living in poverty take responsibility for their younger brothers and sisters. _____
  5 There is very little we can do about poverty in Africa. _____
  6 There are lots of people in Africa willing to foster orphans. _____
  7 Charity donations can help to buy medicines. _____
  8 We can send food to orphaned children. _____

B Listen and follow a discussion

4 **9S.1▶** Listen and decide what's happening in the discussion. Tick ✓ the answer you think is correct.
  a ☐ Two people are describing the same charity organization.
  b ☐ Three people are arguing about the environment.
  c ☐ Two people are trying to persuade their friend to support different charities.

5 Match the speakers with their opinions.
  1 ☐ Stella
  2 ☐ Dmitri
  3 ☐ Donna

  a Charities which help people are more important than environmental ones.
  b The best charities show real results with communities.
  c Charity campaigning is important to governments.

6 Are these expressions agreeing or disagreeing? Write *A* or *D*.
  1 [A] Great idea!
  2 ☐ Good for you, Stella.
  3 ☐ Yes, I suppose so.
  4 ☐ Hang on a minute!
  5 ☐ OK, but …
  6 ☐ Maybe you've got a point.
  7 ☐ That's true.
  8 ☐ I'm with Stella.
  9 ☐ Quite right!
  10 ☐ What's that got to do with it?
  11 ☐ I think you might be right there, Dmitri.
  12 ☐ Exactly!

C Read for detail

7 Read the text quickly and tick ✓ the best title.
a ☐ Our impact on the environment
b ☐ The real price of a gold watch
c ☐ How not to waste water

How many of us realize the true cost of the standard of living we enjoy? Fortunately, we live on a planet that is rich in natural resources. Unfortunately, we probably do not take enough care of those resources. Human activity can have an enormous impact on the environment. A couple of examples will show us how great that impact can be.

THE ARAL SEA SPLITS
In the early 1960s, the Aral Sea in Central Asia was the fourth-biggest lake in the world. By 2004, however, this lake was tragically only a quarter of its original size. What had caused such a drastic change?
  Two large rivers flow into this body of water. In the 1940s, an ambitious government decided to use a lot of water from the rivers for irrigation. Unsurprisingly, the lake started to dry up, because it wasn't receiving enough water. In 1987, it split into two parts: the North Aral Sea and the South Aral Sea.
  Around the year 2000, however, another government took action. The irrigation systems were changed and a dam was built between the North and South Seas. Thankfully, the North Aral Sea level is rising again, fish have returned and the regional environment has improved.

INDONESIAN GOLD MINE CONTAMINATES RIVER
In the south of Spain in 1998, a dam full of toxic mining waste collapsed and seriously contaminated 45 km of river next to a National Park. Luckily, public reaction was very strong, and the damage was repaired. But the world's biggest gold mine – the Grasberg Mine in Eastern Indonesia – has been dumping uncontrolled waste in rivers for 40 years, and will continue to do the same, as there are no environmental agreements in the region. So if you think your gold watch is expensive, just think of the price paid by the land and people who live near the mine!

8 Match the highlighted words with these definitions. Use a dictionary to help you.
1 to divide into two or more parts _____ (vb)
2 the effect something, e.g. a situation or event, has on something else _____ (n)
3 a barrier built across a river or lake to stop water flowing _____ (n)
4 supplying water to an area of land _____ (n)
5 relating to a local area _____ (adj)
6 toxic or poisonous, e.g. not safe to drink _____ (adj)

D Write your opinions

9 Read the discussion about technology, and the blog posts a–c. Decide which blogs:
1 ☐ ☐ Give examples of problems
2 ☐ ☐ Ask questions to one of the other writers
3 ☐ ☐ Discuss solutions to the problems

Does technology really provide solutions?
POSTED BY REDROOSTER ON FEB 4TH.

New discussion
I think technology's fun, but I get a bit scared when I stop to think about it. OK, so the Internet provides communication, and car safety gets better. But when things break down, they cost so much more to repair! Is this really making life easier? I don't think so.

ADD YOUR COMMENTS

Rocinante says: Feb 10th, 4.32 p.m.
a Technology comes from industry. But industry causes pollution. It's true that there are environmental laws and agencies. [1] Fortunately / Unfortunately, for every 'clean' company, there are ten 'dirty' ones. Don't forget disasters like Bhopal in India, where 20,000 people died. [2] Luckily / Incredibly, 25 years later, there are still people who have had no compensation for that.

Roger-dodger says: Feb 15th, 6.49 p.m.
b It seems that you don't appreciate the benefits of technology. [3] Exactly / Clearly, you can only see the bad things. But what about all the helpful inventions? Don't you use mobile phones, cars, and the Internet? Yes, there are problems. We need to recycle much more, and we need to use cleaner energy. [4] Fortunately / Unfortunately, though, technology is working on these things too: biofuels, alternative energies, biodegradable materials – these things are already with us!

Hayley says: Feb 16th, 9.13 p.m.
c I think you both have valid arguments. To my mind, however, there's another key question here. What kind of solution is a virtual world like Second Life, or the Internet? [5] Luckily / Clearly these things are popular, but I'm not sure they're very 'helpful'. Isn't this 'solution' just an escape from the real world? I'm so busy in real life that I don't have time for a virtual life – [6] thankfully! / incredibly!

10 Underline the correct attitude adverbs 1–6 in the texts.

11 Write your own comment on the blog.

Now try the Self check on >> p.84.

How to **exchange opinions**

G articles *the, a, an*   V shops; agreeing and disagreeing

10A

A Vocabulary shops

1 Complete the word puzzle. What can you buy in the extra shop at number 8?

Where do I go to find … ?
1 my *PC Weekly* magazine
2 a birthday cake
3 the new Ken Follett novel for Mum
4 Grandad's medicines
5 new boots for Fred
6 beef sausages for dinner
7 a place with lots of different shops selling clothes, toys, birthday presents, etc.

2 Complete the sentences with these words.

~~dry cleaner's~~   optician's   clothes shops   department store
laundrette   high-street shops   library   bank

1 **A** I need my suit cleaned.
  B Try the _dry cleaner's_ near the bank.
2 **A** I need a new pair of glasses.
  B The _____ is in Market Street.
3 **A** My mother wants me to buy a set of towels.
  B The best place is the _____ in the town centre.
4 **A** I have a bag of clothes to be washed.
  B There's a _____ just round the corner.
5 **A** I have to cash a cheque.
  B Well, there's a _____ in the middle of Oxford Street.
6 **A** My friend asked me to return these books for him.
  B Then you'll need the _____. It's just next to the bus station.
7 **A** In my opinion, the service in _____ is friendlier than in shopping malls.
  B But if you're interested in fashion, there are so many more _____ to choose from in the big shopping centres.

B Grammar articles *the, a, an*

3 Underline the correct article.
  A Excuse me! Can you help? I think I'm lost.
  B Oh yes? What's ¹ a/the problem?
  A Well, I'm looking for ² a/the Chatham Country Hotel.
  B Right, well, you **are** a bit lost! Let me think. Drive back ³ a/the way you came, until you get to ⁴ a/the big roundabout.
  A Is that ⁵ a/the roundabout with a big tree in the middle?
  B Yes, it's about ten minutes. Then at ⁶ a/the roundabout, take ⁷ a/the second road on the right.
  A Uh-huh.
  B Follow that road for about 6 km. You'll go past ⁸ a/the petrol station and ⁹ a/the restaurant, then you'll see ¹⁰ a/the hotel on the right.
  A Thanks very much! I hope I can remember all that!

4 Complete the text with *the*, *a*, or *an*.

Welcome to **Dunning**!

Dunning is ¹_____ small village about 60 miles north of Glasgow. ²_____ village has ³_____ population of about 800, who live and work mainly on farms. There's ⁴_____ small hotel in ⁵_____ centre, and a few shops on ⁶_____ High Street. There's also ⁷_____ garage on ⁸_____ east side of the village. Visitors can enjoy relaxing walks in ⁹_____ local area, and many like to visit ¹⁰_____ village church, which was built in ¹¹_____ 12th century.

And you? Write about your home town.

1 Where do you live? _____
2 Describe the town's geographical location. _____
3 What kind of town is it? _____
4 What is it famous for? _____
5 What kind of occupations do people have there? _____

How well can you exchange opinions now?
Go back to the **Student's Book** >> p.97 and tick ✓ the line again.

How to talk about your shopping habits   10B

G quantifiers   V packaging   P of

A Vocabulary packaging

1 Complete the gaps with *a*, *o*, *u*, or *i* and write eleven packaging words.

packet
_____
_____
_____
_____
_____
_____
_____
_____
_____
_____

2 Complete the shopping list with the correct form of a word from exercise 1.

1 six _____ of crisps.
2 two _____ of mineral water.
3 three _____ of chocolates.
4 a _____ of lemonade.
5 four _____ of orange juice.
6 a _____ of honey.
7 a _____ of toothpaste.
8 four _____ of pineapple.
9 two _____ of ice cream.
10 three _____ of shopping.

B Pronunciation *of*

3 **10B.1** Listen and check exercise 2.

4 How is *of* pronounced? Listen again and repeat the list.

C Grammar quantifiers

5 Tick ✓ the sentences where the alternatives mean the same.
1 ☐ The meal had a little/enough salt.
2 ☐ They have little/don't have much money.
3 ☐ There were a few/too few biscuits on the plate.
4 ☐ There are too many/a lot of eggs.
5 ☐ I saw very few/hardly any sausages in the fridge.
6 ☐ There's very little/not much oil in the can.

6 Complete the sentences with a suitable quantifier. Use the chart to help you.

a lot of
enough
no
not many
not much
very few
very little

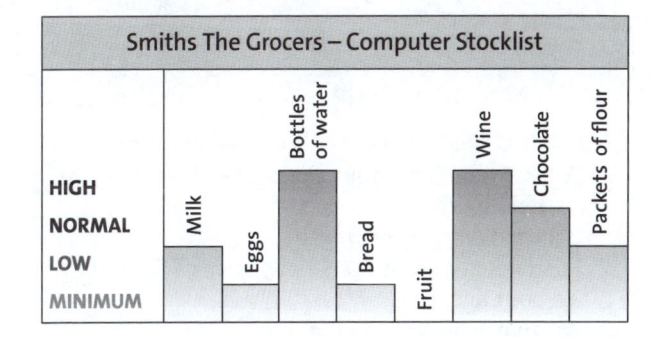

Smiths The Grocers – Computer Stocklist

HIGH / NORMAL / LOW / MINIMUM
Milk, Eggs, Bottles of water, Bread, Fruit, Wine, Chocolate, Packets of flour

1 There is _not much_ milk.
2 There are _____ eggs.
3 There are _____ bottles of water.
4 There's _____ bread.
5 There's _____ fruit.
6 There's _____ wine.
7 There's _____ chocolate.
8 There are _____ packets of flour.

And you? What kind of food shopper are you?
1 I buy a lot of _____, because _____.
2 I don't buy much _____, because _____.
3 I buy very little _____, because _____.
4 I buy very few _____, because _____.

How well can you talk about your shopping habits now?
Go back to the Student's Book >> p.99 and tick ✓ the line again.

How to **talk about recent activities**

G present perfect continuous   V approximate times and amounts   P when to stress *have / has*

A Vocabulary approximate times and amounts

1 Underline the correct time expression.

1 Have you read any good books *lately / or so*?
2 I've lived here *almost / recently* six years.
3 He's *recently / almost* been promoted.
4 I expect the journey will take an hour *almost / or so*.
5 She's read 600 pages, *more or less / about*.
6 How far away is the theatre? *About / lately* ten miles.
7 We've been waiting for this concert for *month / months*.
8 David! We haven't seen you for *ages / times*!

2 Complete the sentences with a suitable time expression.

1 **A** How long have your clothes been hanging on that chair?
   B Five days, *more or less*.
2 I arrived at 8.00. It's 9.15 now, so yes, _____ an hour ago.
3 **A** What have you been doing _____?
   B Not much, really. You?
4 I'm hoping to finish my project in two weeks' _____.
5 **A** Is it far to the hotel?
   B I'd say it's _____ 5 km, certainly not more.
6 He lived in Paris for six years _____, before returning to Norway.

B Grammar present perfect continuous

3 Match the questions and answers.

1 [d] What have the kids been doing?
2 [ ] How long has he been playing on the computer?
3 [ ] How many emails have you written today?
4 [ ] How long have you been studying Japanese?
5 [ ] You look terrible! What have you been doing?
6 [ ] Have you done much exercise recently?

a Since he got up at 10.00!
b Yes, lots. I've been cycling about 30 km a day!
c I've been studying all night.
d ~~Playing in the garden.~~
e Fifteen or so.
f Since I got this job in Tokyo three months ago.

4 Underline the correct tense to complete the rules. Use the questions in exercise 3 to help you.

a We usually use the present perfect *simple / continuous* with questions which ask *how long*?
b We usually use the present perfect *simple / continuous* with questions which ask *how much / many*?

5 Complete the sentences with the verb in the present perfect simple or continuous.

1 He *'s been waiting* (wait) all his life for his dream princess – and he's 84!
2 She _____ (watch) three films in the last four days.
3 He _____ (finish) two lots of homework, and he's got three more to do!
4 I _____ (only / drive) since last April.
5 They _____ (not show) me the photographs of the wedding yet.
6 Police _____ (look) for the suspect for over two years.

C Pronunciation when to stress *have / has*

6 10C.1▶ Predict and underline the stress in the rhyme. Listen and check.

It's been raining
It hasn't been sunny
It's been freezing
It hasn't been funny
Have I been waiting?
I've been waiting for summer.

7 Listen again and repeat the rhyme. Copy the stress patterns.

How well can you talk about recent activities now?
Go back to the Student's Book >> p.101 and tick ✓ the line again.

How to ask about products in a shop

10D

g time and conditional clauses v words connected with buying and selling

A Vocabulary words connected with buying and selling

1 Write the correct words next to the definitions.

1 Give money to someone in exchange for an object or service.   p a y
2 Use your money to buy goods and services, or use your time doing an activity.   _ p _ _ _ _
3 When we want to find out the price, we ask how much something _ _ s _ _.
4 Sometimes an article is less expensive than it originally was, so we say it is r _ _ _ _ _ _ _.
5 Restaurant customers often complain that service is not _ _ c _ _ _ _ _ _ in the prices on the menu.
6 Electrical appliances usually have a two-year _ u _ _ _ t _ _, so you can get free repairs if something goes wrong.
7 The small, printed paper you get from a shop when you buy something.   r _ _ _ _ _ _
8 These supply power to make electrical things work.   b _ _ _ _ _ _ _ _ s
9 When you don't have to pay for something, we say it's _ _ e _.
10 The amount of money a shop asks you to pay for something.   _ _ _ c _

2 Complete the advert with the correct words from exercise 1.

SALE - SALE - SALE!!!

Last year this computer was £1,000 – NOW [1] *reduced* to only £400!

Operates on powerful [2] _____, giving 2 hours of non-stop use.*

3-month [3] _____ for repair or replacement of screen and keyboard. **

Attractive case completely [4] _____.

If you want to buy laptops at the best possible [5] _____, don't [6] _____ any more time looking! At BRIGGS you [7] _____ more or less what the laptops [8] _____ at the factory!

* Batteries not [9] _____.
** For any kind of complaint, our customers must be able to show a [10] _____.

B Grammar time and conditional clauses

3 Underline the correct answer.

1 I'll go shopping unless/**when** I know what I want.
2 She won't buy new shoes unless/until the sales.
3 He'll get that new video game as soon as/as long as it comes out.
4 I won't buy clothes if/until I know they're second-hand.
5 We'll decide what to buy as long as/as soon as they tell us when we can move into the flat.
6 What will you do if/when you don't get paid in time?
7 I don't mind paying a bit more, as long as/unless it's a quality product.
8 I'm not buying a new car as long as/unless this one breaks down!

4 Complete the conversation at Briggs' computer store. Use the correct form of the verbs, and add any other necessary words.

A Good morning, sir! Can I help you?
B I bought this laptop here last month, and it doesn't work properly!
A What exactly is the problem?
B [1] If I /use /more than 30 minutes /battery /not work.
   If I use it for more than 30 minutes, the battery doesn't work.
A I see. Have you had any other problems?
B Yes, I have. [2] It /not play music /unless /switch off /word processor
   _____.
A Right! Anything else?
B [3] As soon as you /click 'Save' /screen /go blank
   _____.
A Fine. [4] We /check all that /as long as /you /have receipt
   _____.
B Yes, yes. Here's the receipt. How long will it take?
A [5] We /not know that /until /we /have a look /sir
   _____.
B But I've got some very urgent work to do!
A [6] We /lend /you another one /until /yours /repaired
   _____.
B Ah, that would be very helpful.

How well can you ask about products in a shop now?
Go back to the Student's Book >> p.103 and tick ✓ the line again.

61

Unit 10 Skills Practice

A Read a problem page letter

1 Read the text quickly. Where do you think it is from?
   a ☐ a financial newspaper
   b ☐ a consumer magazine
   c ☐ a shopping catalogue

People tell me that I have a problem with shopping. And maybe I have been spending more time shopping lately. I mean, I go to the mall every weekend, and maybe once or twice in the week as well. The shop windows are really great – there's always something different to see. And it's true that I pick up a few things when I'm there.

But then there are the sales as well. I can't resist shopping for bargains in the sales. My wife tells me we don't need all those things, but they're so cheap and such good quality … 'Don't go shopping unless you can control your spending!' she says. But we've reached the point where she's been threatening to get my credit card cancelled. Life's getting tough!

Bill, Hackney

This sounds like a case of compulsive shopping, and hundreds, maybe thousands, of people share the same obsession. I'm afraid there's no easy solution, although there are a number of options we can recommend.

One thing you could do is to try making a list before you go out. You won't buy so many things if you think first about what you really need.

Another good idea would be to check your budget. How much can you afford to spend? If you can't control your money, don't take your credit card with you! For example, take a £50 note and say: 'I can buy what I want, as long as it doesn't cost more than £50.' (Obviously you can only do this once a week, or once a month!)

Lastly, if you still can't control things, maybe you should just avoid going to the shops. There's a lot more to life than just shopping. Instead of spending your family's income, spend time with them. Be sociable! Take up a hobby, go cycling or swimming, or go out with your friends. But let someone else do the shopping.

Angela, our financial expert

2 Read the text more carefully, then write *true*, *false* or *doesn't say*.
   1 Bill goes to the shops more than once a week.
      True
   2 He buys less at the sales than during the week.
      _____
   3 His wife has had enough of her husband's bad habit.
      _____
   4 Compulsive shopping is not a very common problem.
      _____
   5 A list usually helps to reduce the amount you spend.
      _____
   6 Social contacts will only make you spend more.
      _____

B Listen to people debating a topic

3 10S.1▶ Listen to the conversation between Bill and Ruth. Which topic are they debating?
   a ☐ Bill's spending habit
   b ☐ who does the shopping
   c ☐ money for the holidays

4 What do Bill and Ruth agree and disagree on? Write *A* or *D*.
   1 ☐D☐ keeping the mirrors for the children.
   2 ☐ that Bill promised not to buy shoes
   3 ☐ that Bill's sister is crazy
   4 ☐ that Bill had a problem
   5 ☐ that Bill is spending less than before
   6 ☐ that Bill still has a bit of a problem

5 Correct the sentences with information from the conversation.
   1 The mirrors were two for the price of one.
      _____
   2 Bill bought three pairs of shoes last week.
      _____
   3 Bill's sister gave him money to buy shoes.
      _____
   4 Last year, Bill spent the rent money on shopping.
      _____
   5 Bill feels depressed if he stays at home.
      _____

C Read for style

6 Read the first paragraph of the letter quickly. Which description is accurate?
- a ☐ It's a letter to a consumer magazine about a bad purchase.
- b ☐ It's a recommendation on a website for other readers.
- c ☐ It's a formal letter of complaint to the manager of a shop.

Dear Sir,

I am writing to express my dissatisfaction with a product I purchased recently from your shop. I bought an MP3 player, but after only three weeks the volume no longer works correctly.

My receipt is dated March 12th and the model reference is siMP 16/3. By the end of the month, there were problems with the volume control. First, I checked the instructions. Then I tried changing the battery. Finally, I pressed the 'Pause' button. However, I still cannot hear the music at a reasonable volume.

Hopefully, this is enough information for you to send a replacement. I would be grateful if you could do this as soon as possible. Here is my address:

11 Marley Road
Liverpool L6 2NX

Yours faithfully,

E Rowlands

Edward Rowlands

---

7 The second paragraph gives more information about the problem. Find a fact that is not relevant.
_____.

8 The final paragraph calls for action. Which two other things could Edward Rowlands have done to make sure he gets a replacement MP3 player? Tick ✓ the options.
1. ☐ enclosed a receipt with the letter
2. ☐ offered to return the original product
3. ☐ returned the battery that came with the product

D Write a letter of complaint

9 Look at sentences a–f below. What is the writer complaining about?
1. ☐ He ordered a watch but has not received it.
2. ☐ He has been sent the wrong watch.
3. ☐ He is not allowed to exchange the watch.

a I recently ordered the *Onyx Boudoir* watch from your catalogue for my girlfriend's birthday.
b When my girlfriend tried the watch, it was far too big for her.
c The watch I received in the post was a man's watch.
d I enclose a copy of the receipt and expect the correct watch.
e As the error is not mine, I would like you to exchange the watch.
f I telephoned the Customer Service Department, who said I should explain the problem in writing.

10 This is a paragraph plan for a letter of complaint. Which sentences in exercise 9 match the different sections 1–4?

Dear Ms. Kingston,

1 Explaining the problem _____

2 Giving one fact _____

3 Action taken by customer _____

4 Asking for action from Customer Service Department

_____

Yours sincerely,

Robert Butler

---

11 Write a letter of complaint about the watch. Use the completed paragraph plan from exercise 10 and your answers to exercises 7 and 8 to help you.

Now try the Self check on >> p.85.

How to give and ask about directions

11A

G indirect questions V the street

A Vocabulary the street

1 Write the numbers 1–10 from the map next to these places.
   a ☐ bridge
   b ☐ car park
   c ☐ crossroads
   d ☐ dead-end street
   e ☐ path
   f ☐ library
   g ☐ roundabout
   h ☐ T-junction
   i ☐ town hall
   j ☐ taxi rank

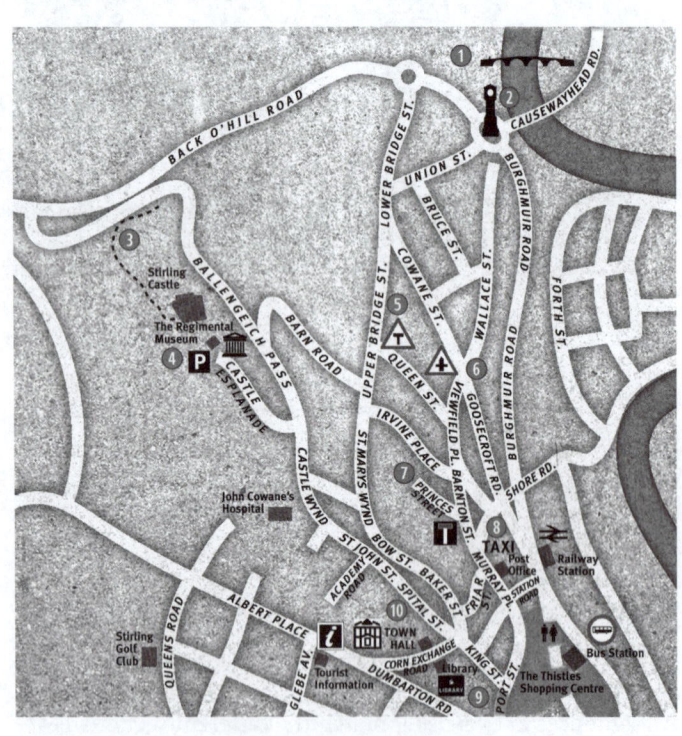

2 Identify these places on the map.
   1 It's a large building between Port Street and Burghmuir Road. _The Thistles Shopping Centre._
   2 It's behind the Regimental Museum. _____
   3 It's in Murray Place, next to the taxi rank. _____
   4 It's at the end of Queens Road. _____
   5 It's on the south side of Corn Exchange Road. _____
   6 It's on Queens Road, just south of the junction with Albert Place. _____
   7 From the Post Office, turn right along Barnton Street, turn left up Irvine Place, cross into Barn Road, and you'll see it at the end of the road. _____
   8 It's opposite the end of Station Road. _____

B Grammar indirect questions

3 Rewrite the questions indirectly. Start with the word provided.
   1 Where's King Street?
     Do you know where King Street is ?
   2 Where's the Post Office?
     Can _____ ?
   3 Where's the tourist information office?
     Do _____ ?
   4 Where's Wallace Street?
     How _____ ?
   5 Is there a car park near here?
     Do _____ ?
   6 Are there any toilets near here?
     Can _____ ?
   7 Is there a bus station near here?
     Do _____ ?
   8 Is the library in Albert Place?
     Can _____ ?

4 Match these answers to the questions in exercise 3. Use the map in exercise 1 to help you.
   a ☐ 3 It's on the corner of Glebe Avenue and Dumbarton Road.
   b ☐ No, it isn't. It's on Corn Exchange Road.
   c ☐ Yes, there's one on the east side of the shopping centre.
   d ☐ Go to the north end of Corn Exchange Road and turn right.
   e ☐ Yes, there's one near the Regimental Museum.
   f ☐ It's south of the roundabout with the clock tower.
   g ☐ Yes, there are several of them in the shopping centre.
   h ☐ It's in Murray Place, just opposite Friars Street.

And you? Write directions for a visitor to your home town.

1 Can you tell me the way to the bus station?
_____

2 Do you know if there's a good hotel near here?
_____

3 Can you tell me where to find a taxi rank?
_____

4 Do you know if I can hire a bicycle?
_____

5 Can you tell me where the nearest petrol station is?
_____

6 Do you know how to get to the high school?
_____

How well can you give and ask about directions now?
Go back to the Student's Book >> p.107 and tick ✓ the line again.

How to **talk about holiday accommodation**

G *to have something done* V *describing holiday accommodation*

11B

A Vocabulary *describing holiday accommodation*

1 Complete the hotel description with the words below.

~~secluded~~ friendly magnificent delicious efficient comfortable elegant

> 🌴 *Paradise Getaway offers you …*
>
> ♦ a(n) ¹ *secluded* location
>   (away from the noise of the town centre)
> ♦ ² _____ views
>   (You can see countryside, the sea and the islands.)
> ♦ a(n) ³ _____ building
>   (original historic castle, decorated by famous designers)
> ♦ ⁴ _____ staff
>   (helpful, patient, always answer your questions)
> ♦ ⁵ _____ service
>   (You never have to wait more than a moment.)
> ♦ ⁶ _____ rooms
>   (new beds, thick carpets, central heating)
> ♦ and of course, ⁷ _____ food!
>   (fresh, well-cooked, full of flavour)
>
> *Book your getaway today!*

2 ~~Cross out~~ the adjectives in the letter which are NOT suitable.

Dear Tamara,

We're just back from the most incredible resort. I couldn't <u>wait</u> to tell you!

The hotel was very ¹ secluded / elegant / ~~delicious~~. The views were lovely, and the sunsets were ² comfortable / delightful / magnificent. They have lots of facilities, and a library which is ³ elegant / delicious / delightful.

And the rooms really were ⁴ comfortable / elegant / friendly. As for the service, it was ⁵ friendly / secluded / efficient. The food was of course absolutely ⁶ delicious / efficient / magnificent. And the local people we met were really ⁷ friendly / delightful / secluded.

Call me in the morning and I'll give you the details. You really <u>must</u> see the place!

Love,
Mum

B Grammar *to have something done*

3 <u>Underline</u> the correct answers.

Henry Strutter is rich. He pays other people to do things for him. Brian Grinder is poor, and he has to do all of the jobs himself.

1 Grinder <u>cleaned the windows</u> / had the windows cleaned.
2 Strutter painted his house / <u>had his house painted</u> by Grinder's son, Michael.
3 Grinder is going to wash his car / have his car washed.
4 Strutter built a swimming-pool / had a swimming-pool built for his daughter, Mabel.
5 Grinder is clearing out the garage / having the garage cleared out.
6 Strutter planted trees / had trees planted in the garden by Grinder's son, Michael.

4 Mabel and Michael fell in love, and Strutter organized their wedding. Write the things he had done.

1 *He had the invitations printed in Berlin.*
   (invitations / print in Berlin)
2 _____
   (dress / make in Paris)
3 _____
   (cake / bake in Rome)
4 _____
   (flowers / send from Costa Rica)
5 _____
   (garden / decorate)
6 _____
   (photos / publish in magazine)

And you? What have you recently had done?

_____
_____
_____
_____

How well can you talk about holiday accommodation now?
Go back to the Student's Book >> p.109 and tick ✓ the line again.

65

How to give health advice

11c

G *have to, need to, should, ought to*   V *health and travel*   P *the main stress in a sentence*

A Vocabulary health and travel

1 Find nine words or phrases related to health and precautions when you travel.

mosquitonetmedicalinsuranceinsectrepellentsunblockinjectionstaidkitmosquitonetmedicalinsuran... (word spiral: mosquito net, medical insurance, insect repellent, sunblock, injections, first aid kit, tap water, emergency, pills)

_____   _____
_____   _____
_____   _____
_____   _____
_____

2 Complete the text with the words and phrases from exercise 1.

> We went on a camping holiday in 2007, and that wasn't too difficult. We took the medicine for Dad's heart problem, and some ¹_____ for Mum, because she always gets bitten. We also took some ²_____ as we've all got very pale skin, and a ³_____ for any small accidents on the way.
>
> But last year we decided to go to Central America, and that was more of a problem. Everybody had to take anti-malaria ⁴_____ a month before leaving. Mum still insisted that we had a ⁵_____ around the bed, 'just to be safe'. Mum also refused to drink the ⁶_____ because she was worried about getting cholera. One of the hotel guests became ill, so maybe she was right after all! But we were OK, because we'd all had our ⁷_____ before leaving.
>
> The only real ⁸_____ was when Dad had a bit of a problem with a shark at the beach, but fortunately we had ⁹_____, so we didn't have to pay at the hospital when they put his leg back on again. Unfortunately, the shark wasn't so lucky!

B Grammar have to, need to, should, ought to

3 Underline the correct words to describe preparations for a day at the beach. Use the chart to help you.

B A day at the beach
M A day in the mountains

	necessary	not necessary	good idea	bad idea
1 sunhat	B	M		
2 extra clothes			B	M
3 sunglasses	B	M		
4 food	M	B		
5 water	B M			
6 mobile phone			M	B
7 map	M	B		
8 book			B	M

A Day at the Beach
1 You have to / don't need to / should wear a sunhat.
2 You need to / don't have to / shouldn't take extra clothes.
3 You need to / don't have to / ought to take sunglasses.
4 You should / don't need to / shouldn't take food.
5 You need to / don't have to / ought to take water.
6 You have to / don't need to / shouldn't take your mobile phone.
7 You need to / don't have to / shouldn't take a map.
8 You have to / don't need to / should take a book.

4 Write sentences for a day in the mountains using *need to / don't need to* and *should / shouldn't*. Use the chart to help you.

1 *You don't need to take a sunhat* .
2 _____ .
3 _____ .
4 _____ .
5 _____ .
6 _____ .
7 _____ .
8 _____ .

C Pronunciation the main stress in a sentence

5 Predict and underline the main stress in these sentences.
   1 Should I take any sun block with me?
   2 Do we need to get some travel insurance?
   3 Will there be accommodation for us?
   4 Did you bring the road maps?
   5 How good is public transport?
   6 What kind of food should I avoid?

6 **11C.1**▶ Listen and check. Repeat and copy the stress.

How well can you give health advice now?
Go back to the Student's Book >> p.111 and tick ✓ the line again.

How to **give extra information**

G non-defining relative clauses   V travel problems   P non-defining relative clauses

A Grammar and Vocabulary travel problems; non-defining relative clauses

1 Match pictures a–f with sentences 1–6.

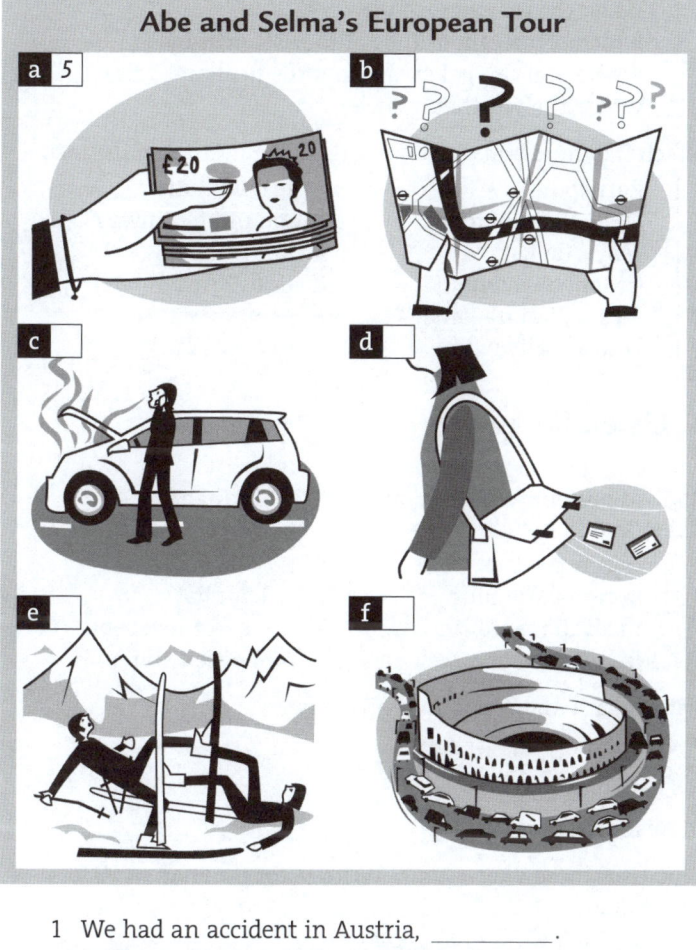

Abe and Selma's European Tour

a 5
b ☐
c ☐
d ☐
e ☐
f ☐

1 We had an accident in Austria, _____.
2 We had a breakdown with Mike, whose car is really old, _____.
3 We got stuck in the traffic in Rome, _____.
4 We lost our way in London, _____.
5 We ran out of money in Milan, _____.
6 We lost our tickets in Germany, _____.

2 Match the relative clauses a–f with the gaps in sentences 1–6 above.
 a ☐ when we were looking for Trafalgar Square
 b ☐ where we visited Munich
 c ☑ when we were skiing
 d ☐ when we were driving around France
 e ☐ when we were shopping with Alice
 f ☐ which is the worst we've ever seen

3 Complete the sentences with the correct form of these verbs.

get ×2   have ×2   leave   lose   miss ×3   run out

Amy and Jack's Disaster Week

1 On Monday, Jack [1] _ran out_ of petrol on the way to see his mother.
2 On Tuesday, Jack [2] _____ his concert ticket, and Amy [3] _____ her train stop and arrived late for a meeting.
3 On Wednesday, Amy [4] _____ stopped for speeding and Jack [5] _____ his wallet on the train.
4 On Thursday, Jack [6] _____ lost on the motorway because he [7] _____ the turning for Derby.
5 On Friday, Amy [8] _____ an accident in the garden and had to go to hospital with Brenda.
6 On Saturday, they [9] _____ a breakdown on the way to the airport and [10] _____ their flight, so on Sunday they decided to stay at home!

4 Match the completed sentences in exercise 3 with these relative clauses to give extra information about Amy and Jack's week.
 a ☐ , who is one of their neighbours.
 b ☐ , when he was coming back from a late night at work.
 c ☐ , which her boss was really angry about.
 d ☐ , where they hope they'll get some rest.
 e ☐ , where he had an appointment with a client.
 f ☐ , whose 80th birthday is next month.

B Pronunciation non-defining relative clauses

5 **11D.1▶** Listen and write a comma in the space when you hear a pause.
 1 She lives near the park____where I used to play.
 2 She lives near the park____where I used to play.
 3 We asked the policeman____who was on the corner.
 4 We asked the policeman____who was on the corner.
 5 I carried the suitcase____which was heavy.
 6 I carried the suitcase____which was heavy.

6 Check your answers in the audio script on ›› p.94. Repeat and copy the pronunciation.

How well can you give extra information now?
Go back to the Student's Book ›› p.113 and tick ✓ the line again.

67

Unit 11 Skills Practice

A Read a tourist brochure

1 Read the text quickly and match the headings with the paragraphs.
   a ☐ Where to stay
   b ☐ How to travel
   c ☐ When to go
   d ☐ What to see and do

Exotic Sri Lanka

1 Sri Lanka has a bit of everything for the visitor. If you want to relax, there are magnificent tropical beaches in the south. If the beach gets too hot for you, however, you can travel inland, ¹_____. Visit the island's historical monuments, ²_____. Go for a walk in the cool tea plantation of Nuwara Eliya or the botanical gardens, ³_____ of the city. Or, if you feel like shopping, visit Ratnapura and see some of the world's finest gems.

2 Most tourists visit the south and west coasts, and the hill country in the centre of the island. The best time for these areas is from December to March, ⁴_____. If you visit between May and August, you can expect monsoon rains most of the time!

3 The island's only airport is just north of Colombo, the capital. There are train services to many parts of the island. If you enjoy travelling by train, don't miss the mountain line from Colombo to Badulla, via Kandy, ⁵_____ on the island. Buses are frequent and inexpensive, but often very crowded. If you can afford to rent a car, this is probably the most comfortable way to get around – as long as you remember to drive on the left!

4 Sri Lanka offers all the usual kinds of accommodation, from luxury hotels to more modest holiday apartments and guest houses. Whether you are travelling alone or in a group, you will find a suitable place at the right price. In July and August, make your reservation well in advance, especially if you plan to visit Kandy or Kataragama, ⁶_____ in the local festivals.

2 Match relative clauses a–f with gaps 1–6 in the text in exercise 1.
   a [5] which is one of the most spectacular trips
   b ☐ where thousands of people take part
   c ☐ when the weather is fairly dry
   d ☐ which attract thousands of tourists every year
   e ☐ where you can get away from the heat and noise
   f ☐ where the weather is cooler

3 Match the times and places with their significance in the text.
   1 [e] Ratnapura   a tea plantation
   2 ☐ December–March   b mountain railway
   3 ☐ May–August   c local festivals
   4 ☐ Colombo–Badulla   d rainy season
   5 ☐ Kandy/Kataragama   e ~~gem town~~
   6 ☐ Nuwara Eliya   f dry season

B Listen for advice

4 **11S.1▶** What will you need on a trip to Sri Lanka? Listen and tick ✓.
   1 ✓ injections   5 ☐ mosquito net
   2 ☐ anti-malaria pills 6 ☐ sun hat
   3 ☐ medical insurance   7 ☐ insect repellent
   4 ☐ first aid kit   8 ☐ bottled water

5 Listen again and check your answers.

6 Find two more suggestions.
   A Don't have _____.
   B Never eat in the _____.

7 Who uses these expressions? Write M for the man or W for the woman.
   1 ☐ Listen, I wanted to ask you …
   2 ☐ Let me just think …
   3 ☐ Is there anything else I should know?
   4 ☐ You can't really be sure …
   5 ☐ That sounds reasonable …
   6 ☐ I hadn't thought of that …

8 For each of the expressions in exercise 7, write Q for question or R for response.
   1 [Q]   2 ☐   3 ☐   4 ☐   5 ☐   6 ☐

C Read and follow events

9 Read the text quickly and say what it is.
a ☐ a letter
b ☐ an online travel blog
c ☐ a magazine article
d ☐ a postcard

Wednesday 12th
Our plane arrived late yesterday, so we had to spend the night in the first hotel we could find, which was a bit expensive. But at least it had air-conditioning. The weather isn't really so hot, but the humidity is high, which makes life uncomfortable. Today we got lost on the way to the bus station! We took a wrong turning somewhere and arrived at a market. Tamara got a bit sunburnt, so we'll do something different tomorrow.

Thursday 13th
Did I say *different*? I wasn't joking! First, we took the train up to Kandy, the old capital. It was slow, it was crowded, but the views were just spectacular! Then we went to see this famous temple which was right beside a lake. Wonderful! Much cooler than at the beach. After that we had lunch in a popular restaurant, where they don't use plates! They serve the food on fresh banana leaves, and you eat with your hand. In the afternoon, we went for a walk in the botanical gardens, where they have the biggest coconut trees I've ever seen. Afterwards, we did some shopping for souvenirs in the town centre. It isn't that cheap, but they have some very nice things there. In the end, we sat on the hotel balcony and watched the full moon over the palm trees. All in all, it was a fantastic day.

---

10 Put Thursday's events in the correct order.
☐ visit the temple
☐ buy souvenirs
☐ see the full moon
☑ train journey
☐ eat in a restaurant
☐ walk in the gardens

11 Can you remember which sequencers go with the answers in exercise 10? Put the words in order. Then check your answers in the text.

after that   afterwards   ~~first~~
in the afternoon   in the end   then

1 *First*_____ 5 _____
2 _____   6 _____
3 _____
4 _____

D Write a tourist recommendation

12 Put the paragraphs A–D of this tourist recommendation in order.

1 ☐   2 ☐   3 ☐   4 ☐

A   This is a very popular tourist destination and can be quite busy sometimes, and unfortunately the weather can also make life difficult. However, it is such a magnificent place that it's definitely worth the effort.

B   One of Sri Lanka's most incredible places to visit is the rock fortress of Sigiriya, which is in the northern part of the island. It's a huge rock about 350 metres high, with the ruins of a fifth-century palace on the top.

C   When you arrive, ¹_____ climb the stairs to the wall paintings, which are about 1,500 years old. ²_____, you continue climbing the iron stairs to the top of the rock. ³_____, it can be very windy, so do take care. From the top you can see the ruins of the fortress, the water tanks, and spectacular views of the island. Take your time to appreciate the building work that happened here. ⁴_____, it's time to go back down the stairs, and catch another bus back to the town.

D   The easiest way to get there is by bus. There is a bus service from the town of Polonnaruwa. You can do the visit in a morning or an afternoon. You should take a sun hat and some water for the heat, but you shouldn't need food, because there is lots available when you're there.

---

13 Put these words in the numbered gaps in the text.
however   finally   first   then

14 Complete the paragraph plan for a special place you can recommend to tourists.

TOURIST RECOMMENDATION

1 where to go, and how to get there _____
   _____

2 things you'll need to take _____
   _____

3 things to see and do _____
   _____

4 possible problems _____
   _____

---

15 Use your notes from exercise 14 to write a recommendation for a web travel forum. Write one paragraph for each section.

Now try the Self check on >> p.86.

How to explain your point of view

12A

G *so, because, (in order) to*   P keeping your turn

A Grammar *so, because, (in order) to*

1 Complete the rules with *so*, *because*, or *in order to*.
 a We use _____ to express the result of actions.
 b We use _____ to indicate the purpose of an action.
 c We use _____ to explain the cause of an action.

2 Underline the correct answers.
 1 A man went to the bank *so*/*to* borrow some money, but the bank said no.
 2 He robbed a shop *so*/*to* get the money he wanted.
 3 The shop owner gave the police a description *so*/*to* they could find the man.
 4 They put the man in jail *so*/*to* make him pay for his crime.
 5 In jail he studied economics *so*/*to* improve his future life.
 6 He wanted to be his own boss, *so*/*to* he started his own business.
 7 He worked very hard *so*/*to* make it successful.
 8 One day he took the company money and disappeared, *so*/*to* now the police are looking for him again.

3 Complete the traditional animal story with *so*, *because*, or *to*.

B Pronunciation keeping your turn

4 **12A.1** Listen to the sentences. Underline where you hear the **long** sound, while the speaker gets more time to think and continue.
 1 I think Bat was very stupid!
 2 I think the birds were too jealous!
 3 It's just like those Aesop stories!
 4 I think the moral is that everyone should know their place.

5 Listen again and repeat. Copy the **long** sound.

And you? Complete the sentences to explain your point of view.

1 I've lived here for ____ years now, so _____.
2 I came to this school to _____.
3 The weather is going to be _____ tomorrow, so _____.
4 Sometimes I get up very _____, because _____.
5 I've worked _____ all year, so _____.
6 I'm saving/spending my money, because _____.
7 I don't think I'll _____.

WHY BATS ONLY COME OUT AT NIGHT

Everyone said that Bat was ugly. He was very unhappy, ¹_____ he flew up ²_____ see God. Bat asked God for lots of feathers, ³_____ he always felt cold. 'But feathers are for birds, not for bats,' God said, ⁴_____ Bat was told he couldn't have any. But then God had an idea: each bird could give Bat one feather, ⁵_____ Bat could then be warm. Bat was very happy and flew everywhere ⁶_____ show everyone his new feathers. But the birds became angry ⁷_____ Bat was becoming arrogant, and they flew up ⁸_____ talk to God. God took away Bat's feathers, ⁹_____ he became cold and ugly again, like before. Now, he only comes out at night ¹⁰_____ look for his feathers, and he flies very fast, ¹¹_____ he doesn't want to be seen.

How well can you explain your point of view now?
Go back to the Student's Book >> p.117 and tick ✓ the line again.

70

How to talk about hopes and wishes

12B

v wish, hope, be glad   P contrastive stress

A Vocabulary wish, hope, be glad

1 Complete Mum's letter to Alf with the correct form of *wish*, *hope*, or *be glad*.

Dear Alf,

Thanks so much for your nice letter. That sounds like a great holiday place you've gone to! I ¹_____ to hear you're having a good time there. How long will you be away? I ²_____ the weather stays sunny for you. Yes, I ³_____ I could be there too, but there's been a lot to do since your dad died, you know. Your sister Ethel's getting married soon, so we all ⁴_____ you'll be back in time for the wedding. I just ⁵_____ your dad was here to see it all. Anyway, Ethel sends her love. She says she's ⁶_____ to hear you've got such great friends where you are, and she ⁷_____ to see you soon. And I ⁸_____ I could talk to you, son. Haven't they got a phone number where you are?

Love,

Mum

2 Write the reality behind Alf's wishes.
   1 I wish I was at home watching TV.
      I'm not at home and I'm not watching TV.
   2 I wish I could tell my mum where I am.
      _____.
   3 I wish the food here was better.
      _____.
   4 I wish I hadn't done the robbery.
      _____.
   5 I wish I didn't have to share a cell with Bert.
      _____.
   6 I wish my girlfriend could visit me.
      _____.
   7 I wish Bert didn't talk in his sleep.
      _____.
   8 I wish they would let me out of here.
      _____.

3 Write Bert's wishes.
   1 It's too cold in here!
      I wish it wasn't so cold in here.
   2 They don't give us enough food.
      _____.
   3 Alf and I got caught during the robbery.
      _____.
   4 Alf doesn't wash every day!
      _____.
   5 Alf never thinks about other people!
      _____.
   6 They won't let me watch the football!
      _____.
   7 I have to do too much exercise!
      _____.
   8 I can't tell my wife where I am!
      _____.

B Pronunciation contrastive stress

4 Predict and underline the stress in B's answers.
   1 A I wish I had a car like yours!
      B Really? I wish I had a boyfriend like yours!
   2 A I wish I didn't work in a shop!
      B Really? I just wish I had a job!
   3 A I hope it doesn't rain tomorrow.
      B Really? I hope it does rain – I don't want to go out.
   4 A I'm glad he's leaving the company!
      B Really? I wish he was staying!

5 **12B.1▶** Listen and repeat. Copy the stress pattern.

And you? What wishes and hopes do you have?

I wish I was/wasn't _____
_____.

I wish I had _____
_____.

I wish I didn't have to _____
_____.

I wish I could _____
_____.

I hope I _____
_____.

I'm glad that _____
_____.

How well can you talk about hopes and wishes now?
Go back to the Student's Book >> p.119 and tick ✓ the line again.

How to describe the plot of a story

12c

G -ing and -ed clauses V stories, books, fiction P well and anyway

A Vocabulary stories, books, fiction

1 Complete the chart with details from the book summaries.

BOOK A
GENRE: adventure
CHARACTERS: Cynthia Bones, Charlie Chan
SETTING: Hong Kong
PLOT: follow the clues to find the ruby

BOOK B
GENRE: h_____
CHARACTERS:
SETTING:
PLOT:

BOOK C
GENRE: s_____ f_____
CHARACTERS:
SETTING:
PLOT:

BOOK D
GENRE: m_____ m_____
CHARACTERS:
SETTING:
PLOT:

A *The Rangoon Ruby*
A Hong Kong bookseller discovers an old letter that gives clues to the location of the Ruby of Rangoon. Cynthia Bones, an archaeologist, is interested — and so is Charlie Chan, the richest art collector in Hong Kong.
Who will find the Ruby first?

B **Ghoulsville**
EMPTY GRAVES, BLOOD ON THE WALLS, BODIES IN THE WOODS …
Have the dead of Ghoulsville come back to look for revenge?

C **SPACE RACE**
An asteroid is travelling fast towards the international space station.
Can the rescue mission get there in time?

D **CASH CRISIS**
Three city bankers are shot dead in six weeks. Inspector Morgan risks his life to find out what's happening.

B Grammar -ing and -ed clauses

2 Underline the correct words.
1 Inspector Morgan learned that all the murdered men worked/working as bankers.
2 The police found the victims sat/sitting in their cars.
3 Inspector Morgan interviewed neighbours worried/worrying by the shots.
4 He received a letter warned/warning him to stop the investigation.
5 The officer helped/helping him was murdered.

3 Join the sentences with an -ing or -ed clause.
1 He's a bookseller. He's living in Hong Kong.
   He's a bookseller living in Hong Kong.
2 He found a letter. The letter is written in Chinese.
   _____.
3 She's an American archaeologist. She's called Cynthia Bones.
   _____.
4 Charlie Chan is an art collector. He knows a lot about precious stones.
   _____.
5 The story begins with Bones. Bones is reading the letter.
   _____.

C Pronunciation well and anyway

4 Complete the sentences with well or anyway.
¹_____, as I was saying, it's a kind of science-fiction story, and it takes place on this strange planet. ²_____, there's a group of survivors who …

³_____, I suppose this is a horror story. It starts off with these dead bodies in a car. ⁴_____, the hero and his girlfriend have to escape …

5 **12C.1▶** Listen, check, and repeat. Pay special attention to the intonation.

And you? Complete the sentences.
The last book I read was called _____.
It was a _____ story, set in _____.
The main characters are _____.
The plot is _____.

How well can you describe the plot of a story now?
Go back to the Student's Book >> p.121 and tick ✓ the line again.

How to talk about important decisions   12D

G 3rd conditional   P would have

A Grammar 3rd conditional

A truck carrying supermarket supplies fell off a bridge yesterday and hit a train. Six people died in the accident, including the truck driver. Experts say the accident was probably caused by the very bad weather conditions.

1 Read the newspaper report about an accident, then complete parts b and c in the following sentences.
   a what actually happened
   b what we imagine later
   c the consequence

   1 a The weather was really bad.
      b If the weather _hadn't been_ so bad,
      c _the accident wouldn't have happened._ (not happen)
   2 a The train was late.
      b If the train _____ on time,
      c it _____ the truck. (not hit)
   3 a I forgot my bag, so I missed the train.
      b If I _____ my bag,
      c I _____ on that train. (be)
   4 a I saw the accident.
      b If I _____ the accident,
      c I _____. (not believe it)
   5 a The train wasn't full.
      b If the train _____ full,
      c there _____ a major tragedy. (be)
   6 a The driver lost control.
      b If the driver _____ control,
      c nobody _____ here. (die)
   7 a The safety barriers on the bridge were weak.
      b If the barriers _____ stronger,
      c the truck _____ off it. (not fall)

2 Rewrite the story using 3rd conditionals.

   1 Mike Perry felt depressed because he'd lost his job.
      If he hadn't lost his job, _he wouldn't have felt depressed_.
   2 He went on an exotic holiday because he felt depressed.
      If _____, _____.
   3 He met a pretty girl when he was at the beach.
      If _____, _____.
   4 He fell in love, so they decided to fly back together.
      They _____ if _____.
   5 He carried a bag for her. He didn't know it contained drugs.
      He _____ if _____.
   6 She lied to the police, and he went to prison.
      He _____ if _____.

B Pronunciation would have

3 Complete the sentences with would have / wouldn't have.
   I ¹_____ waited if you'd asked.
   I ²_____ called if you'd waited.
   I ³_____ written if you'd replied.
   But you ⁴_____ asked
   You ⁵_____ waited
   And you ⁶_____ replied
   So now you know why
   I didn't wait or call or write.

4 12D.1▶ Listen, check, and repeat. Are the positive or negative forms stressed?

   And you? Think about the important decisions in your life and what would have happened, if you'd acted differently.

   | If I hadn't _____, I would have _____. |
   | If I'd _____, I wouldn't have _____. |
   | I would have _____ if _____. |
   | I wouldn't have _____ if _____. |

How well can you talk about important decisions now?
Go back to the Student's Book >> p.123 and tick ✓ the line again.

Unit 12 Skills Practice

A Read a story with a moral

1 Read the story quickly, and put the paragraphs in order.
1 ☐ 2 ☐ 3 ☐ 4 ☐

A Three months later, they visited the building site again, and saw machines moving the earth. After another month, they saw the basic structures of the houses. Two weeks after that, they saw a TV report on a construction scandal, with photographs of the disappeared agent and builder, wanted by the police. But there was no news of all the money that 50 families had paid in advance.

B They found an advert in the local newspaper and went to see an estate agent, a smartly-dressed middle-aged man. If they wanted a quality home at a reasonable price, he said, they had come to the right place. He showed them the plans for a new housing development on the edge of town, in a secluded area away from the main roads. He took them to the site to meet the builder personally. The Smiths were very happy, and paid half the cost of the house in advance.

C In the end, the Smiths realized that they had been tricked. The story shows that you have to be very careful who you trust, especially with your money.

D The Smiths had lived in a rented flat for ten years. It was a spacious flat on the fourth floor, overlooking a park full of trees. But it was also very noisy because of the traffic. So they decided to look for their own house, without so many neighbours or so much noise.

2 Label the paragraphs with these functions.
Action   Moral   ~~Situation~~   Result
1 _Situation_   2 _____   3 _____   4 _____

3 Tick ✓ the best moral for the story.
a ☐ People in glass houses shouldn't throw stones.
b ☐ A bird in the hand is worth two in the bush.
c ☐ Never judge a book by its cover.

4 Correct these sentences about the text.
1 The Smiths' current flat was very noisy because of the people in the park.
The Smiths' flat was noisy because of the traffic.

2 They wanted to find somewhere with nicer neighbours.
_____.

3 The agent they met was in his 60s.
_____.

4 They met the agent, but not the builder.
_____.

5 When they visited the housing development again, the builder had half-built the houses.
_____.

6 Building work on the houses never started.
_____.

7 They discovered they'd been tricked three months after paying their money.
_____.

8 About 50 families were going to pay money when their houses were completed.
_____.

B Listen and follow events

5 12S.1▶ Listen to three speakers talking about how their lives changed. Which speaker (write Caroline, Jeff or Lizzy) is describing an important moment in:
a their personal life   _____
b their education   _____
c their job   _____

6 Match the speaker's name to the description.
1 _____ met an extraordinary teacher.
2 _____ fell in love with a classmate.
3 _____ lives between two countries.
4 _____ worked with computers.
5 _____ has written six books.
6 _____ had to adapt to a different climate.
7 _____ didn't do very well at school.
8 _____ didn't want to work in industry or teaching.
9 _____ has a partner who is ten years older.

C Read and understand the main ideas

7 Read the text quickly and match the paragraphs with the descriptions.
- a ☐ what the man learned
- b ☐ what happened one summer
- c ☐ the consequences
- d ☐ the man and his character

---

1 Daniel Dyson was an [1] *important politician* in the capital city. He was responsible for the city's public transport. In front of the [2] _____, he always advised people to use the bus, the train or the metro. In his personal life, however, he travelled everywhere in a [3] _____, and used his power to avoid paying [4] _____. He enjoyed the good life, eating in [5] _____ in the fashionable parts of the city. Dyson often wrote in the press, defending [6] _____ and criticizing [7] _____ for causing pollution and for driving carelessly.

2 Last summer, Daniel Dyson took his family to a rented house on the coast, where the family stayed for a month. One evening, Dyson went to a party at a friend's house, 20 miles away. At four o'clock in the morning, when he was driving back to his holiday home, Dyson lost control of his car, hit a motorcyclist, and drove into a shop window. Soon afterwards, police found him sitting in the car, with the shop alarm ringing and alcohol in his blood.

3 After the accident, Dyson lost his driving licence for a year, [8] but / so he had to travel to work by public transport. He also had to attend special classes [9] because / in order to get his driving licence back. A lot of people criticized him [10] because / so he had driven so carelessly.

4 Daniel Dyson still writes in the newspapers. The difference is that now, [11] in the end / as a result of his experiences, he actually knows what he's talking about!

---

8 Complete the first paragraph of the story with these phrases.

big car   car drivers   expensive restaurants
public transport   ~~important politician~~   traffic fines
TV cameras

9 When did these events happen? Write the time expressions from paragraph 2.
1. Dyson went to the coast with his family _____
2. He went to a party _____
3. He had a car accident _____
4. The police found him _____

10 Underline the correct connectors in paragraphs 3 and 4.

D Write a story with a moral

11 Complete the sentences with these connectors.

~~at first~~   autumn   but   so   afterwards
because   in order to x2   a year after

1. An ambitious young man got a job in a company.
2. *At first*, he was quite happy, but soon he wanted more.
3. He wasn't very good at his job, _____ he was good-looking, so he started going out with the boss's daughter, Eva.
4. A year later, he married Eva _____ move up in the company.
5. Soon _____, he was made a company director, with a big house and fast cars. But he wasn't happy with Eva.
6. One _____, he met and fell in love with another woman, Elena.
7. He couldn't live without Elena, _____ he divorced Eva and remarried.
8. He lost his job, his house, and the cars _____ of the scandal that followed.
9. _____ the scandal, Elena left him because he didn't have any money.
10. In the end, he was back to where he had started. He had to find a new job, _____ pay the rent.

12 Complete the outline of the story by adding information about the main events.

Situation: ambitious man got job
Action: married the boss's daughter, Eva
Result: was made a company director

Situation: fell in love with another woman
Action: _____
Result: lost his job and house because of the scandal

Situation: _____
Action: Elena left him because of this
Result: _____

13 Choose a moral for the story.
- a Don't put all of your eggs in one basket.
- b Don't bite the hand that feeds you.
- c Don't throw the baby out with the bath water.

14 Write the complete story from your notes, adding any other details you would like.

Now try the Self check on >> p.87.

Unit 1 Self check

Grammar

1 Tick ✓ or correct the sentences.
1. ☐ We email each other every day.
2. ☐ He doesn't need help. He can do his homework by him.
3. ☐ Come on Rachel, let's introduce ourself to the new teacher.
4. ☐ Come to the party tonight. Don't stay at home by you self.
5. ☐ My parents are painting their house themselves.

2 <u>Underline</u> the correct words to complete the sentences.
1. Nicolas wants/is wanting to wake the dog – he is touching it with his foot.
2. Jose Nieto holds/is holding something in his hand – I think it's a book.
3. Maria and Isabel spend a lot of time with the princess. They help/are helping her now.
4. Marcela and the bodyguard talk/are talking about something. They work for the king.
5. I like/am liking Las Meninas – I am writing an essay about it for my class.

Vocabulary

3 Complete the sentences with a suitable word.
1. Sam is a w _ _ _ _ _ _. His wife died five years ago.
2. Wanda isn't married. She's s _ _ _ _ _.
3. My sister has three children, so I have two nephews and one n _ _ _ _.
4. My mum and dad are d _ _ _ _ _ _ _ and both of them have remarried.
5. Alison shares an apartment with her f _ _ _ _ _ _ _ Laura. They're best friends.
6. My n _ _ _ _ _ _ _ _ is from Italy. She's lived next door to us for about ten years.

4 Correct the sentences. The mistake is <u>underlined</u>.
1. I bought lots of fruit in the market: apples, bananas, and <u>pairs</u>.
2. This is the best <u>flower</u> for making bread.
3. Margaret has lost a lot of <u>wait</u>: five kilos!
4. I got the train from Barcelona to Madrid but Anita <u>flu</u> with Air Iberia.
5. Tony <u>road</u> across the USA on his bike.
6. The baby <u>through</u> his toys out of the car.

Pronunciation

5 Match the following letters with the words that have the same vowel sound.

G I K O Q R X

1. ☐ dress /e/
2. ☐ boat /əʊ/
3. ☐ wait /eɪ/
4. ☐ car /ɑː/
5. ☐ drive /aɪ/
6. ☐ you /uː/
7. ☐ three /iː/

Check your answers on >> p.88

What are you going to do now?
a Nothing. I'm happy.
b Revise grammar/vocabulary/pronunciation and try again.
c Ask another student/my teacher for help.

To revise, go to:
Student's Book Review >> p.15   Grammar Bank >> p.136
Workbook >> pp.4–7   www.oup.com/elt/result

Reading

Read these texts again.
Workbook >> p.8 exercise 1
Workbook >> p.9 exercise 7

How confident are you?
I can understand ...
☐ some words
☐ with help
☐ when I read again
☐ everything

Listening

Listen to this audio again.
Workbook >> p.8 audio script **1S.1**▶

How confident are you?
I can understand ...
☐ some words
☐ with help
☐ when I listen again
☐ everything

Writing

Do this writing exercise again.
Workbook >> p.9 exercise 12

How confident are you?
I can write ...
☐ with help
☐ on my own
☐ with some mistakes
☐ with no mistakes

What are you going to do now?
a Nothing. I'm happy.
b Ask my teacher for help.
c Practise my reading/listening/writing.

To practise go to ...
Student's Book >> pp.6–14
Workbook >> pp.8–9
MultiROM Listening section
www.oup.com/elt/result

76 Self checks

Unit 2 Self check

Grammar

1 Tick ✓ or correct the sentences.
  1 ☐ Tourists go rarely to this area.
  2 ☐ They hard ever go shopping.
  3 ☐ They always want to see Big Ben.
  4 ☐ They often quite miss Trafalgar Square.
  5 ☐ They want usually to see the sights.

2 Match the beginnings and endings of the sentences.
  1 ☐ During my first week in Japan, I didn't go out much
  2 ☐ My new friends explained how to use the chopsticks,
  3 ☐ My cold was not quite finished,
  4 ☐ I noticed a person at the next table
  5 ☐ The bowl of water was hot
  a and I started drinking it before it got cold.
  b because I had a terrible cold.
  c and my nose was running a little.
  d and I was soon eating Japanese-style like a native.
  e was looking at me strangely.

Vocabulary

3 Complete the sentences with these words.
  Muslim   Christian   the Middle East   the South Pacific   Central America
  1 Guatemala is in _____.
  2 Jordan, Saudi Arabia and Egypt are in _____.
  3 New Zealand is in _____.
  4 Most people in Morocco are _____.
  5 Most people in Italy are _____.

4 Correct the spelling of the words in the sentences.
  1 The leg is wide at the bottom and narro at the top.
  2 This item is a kind of glove made of lether.
  3 This item has a wooden handel.
  4 The balls contain air so they flote.
  5 This is a round contener made of dried gourd.

Pronunciation

5 Look at the consonant in **bold**. Tick the correct pronunciation.
  1 The Pa**c**ific Ocean   ☐ /k/   ☐ /s/
  2 The Ar**c**tic Ocean   ☐ /k/   ☐ /s/
  3 Catholi**c**   ☐ /k/   ☐ /s/
  4 gara**g**e   ☐ /g/   ☐ /dʒ/
  5 reli**g**ious   ☐ /g/   ☐ /dʒ/
  6 ma**g**azine   ☐ /g/   ☐ /dʒ/

Check your answers on >> p.88

What are you going to do now?
  a Nothing. I'm happy.
  b Revise grammar/vocabulary/pronunciation and try again.
  c Ask another student/my teacher for help.

To revise, go to:
Student's Book Review >> p.25   Grammar Bank >> p.137
Workbook >> pp.10–13   www.oup.com/elt/result

Reading

Read these texts again.
  Workbook >> p.14 exercise 1
  Workbook >> p.15 exercise 8

How confident are you?
I can understand ...
  ☐ some words
  ☐ with help
  ☐ when I read again
  ☐ everything

Listening

Listen to this audio again.
  Workbook >> p.14 audio script **2S.1**

How confident are you?
I can understand ...
  ☐ some words
  ☐ with help
  ☐ when I listen again
  ☐ everything

Writing

Do this writing exercise again.
  Workbook >> p.15 exercise 13

How confident are you?
I can write ...
  ☐ with help
  ☐ on my own
  ☐ with some mistakes
  ☐ with no mistakes

What are you going to do now?
  a Nothing. I'm happy.
  b Ask my teacher for help.
  c Practise my reading/listening/writing.

To practise go to ...
Student's Book >> pp.16–24
Workbook >> pp.14–15
MultiROM Listening section
www.oup.com/elt/result

Unit 3 Self check

Grammar

1 Underline the correct words.

Kimani Ng'ang'a from Kenya, aged 85, is the world's oldest primary school pupil. Kimani [1]started/has started at primary school last year. He [2]didn't go/hasn't gone to school as a child because his family couldn't pay the fees. Kimani is only in his second year but he [3]achieved/has achieved a lot since he started. In the 1950s, Kimani [4]fought/has fought for independence for Kenya but now he is learning to write. He [5]already learnt/has already learnt to write a few words of Swahili.

2 Put the words in brackets in the correct place.
1 I'm looking my baby brother this afternoon. (after)
2 Don't worry about the dishes. I'll wash them today. (up)
3 The story wasn't true. I made up. (it)
4 Can you the music up? I can't hear it. (turn)
5 The shoes were really uncomfortable so I took off. (them)

Vocabulary

3 What is it? Write the school words for each of these descriptions.
1 The teacher writes on it in front of the students. b_____
2 It is a school subject where you learn about the past. h_____
3 It is the time in the middle of the school day when children stop working and play for a short time. b_____
4 It is the teacher's favourite student. t_____ p_____
5 At school, children eat lunch in it. c_____

4 Complete the sentences with these words.

classes   college   lecturer   Masters   professor

1 The head of the department is a _____ of Physics. He's a world-famous expert.
2 I've just finished my degree and I've started work as a _____ in French.
3 After I got my first degree, I then took a _____.
4 I did my A-levels at a further education _____.
5 Dino didn't learn German at school. He studied it during evening _____.

Pronunciation

5 Complete the table with these words.

achievement   application   ~~beautiful~~   chemistry   colourful education   happily   photography   successful   technology

•●•	•●••	•●••	••●•
beautiful			

Check your answers on >> p.88

What are you going to do now?
a Nothing. I'm happy.
b Revise grammar/vocabulary/pronunciation and try again.
c Ask another student/my teacher for help.

To revise, go to:
Student's Book Review >> p.35   Grammar Bank >> p.138
Workbook >> pp.16–19   www.oup.com/elt/result

Reading

Read these texts again.
Workbook >> p.20 exercise 1
Workbook >> p.21 exercise 4

How confident are you?
I can understand …
☐ some words
☐ with help
☐ when I read again
☐ everything

Listening

Listen to this audio again.
Workbook >> p.20 audio script **3S.1**

How confident are you?
I can understand …
☐ some words
☐ with help
☐ when I listen again
☐ everything

Writing

Do this writing exercise again.
Workbook >> p.21 exercise 9

How confident are you?
I can write …
☐ with help
☐ on my own
☐ with some mistakes
☐ with no mistakes

What are you going to do now?
a Nothing. I'm happy.
b Ask my teacher for help.
c Practise my reading/listening/writing.

To practise go to …
Student's Book >> pp.26–34
Workbook >> pp.20–21
MultiROM Listening section
www.oup.com/elt/result

Unit 4 Self check

Grammar

1 For each of the sentences below tick ✓ the correct option, A or B.
   1 a ☐ I first saw BASE jumping in 2005. It looked amazed.
      b ☐ I first saw BASE jumping in 2005. It looked amazing.
   2 a ☐ I was fascinated by the photos of bodybuilders I saw in magazines.
      b ☐ I was fascinating by the photos of bodybuilders I saw in magazines.
   3 a ☐ People think sudoku is a bored mathematical puzzle.
      b ☐ People think sudoku is a boring mathematical puzzle.

2 Complete the text with these words.
   best   popular   easily   convenient   cheaper

   The guitar is ¹_____ than the piano to buy and it's a lot smaller so it's more ²_____ if you live in a small flat. Also you can carry it much more ³_____ so it's better if you move around a lot. On the other hand the piano is probably the ⁴_____ instrument of all for learning music. You can see all of the notes a bit more clearly than you can on the guitar. If a piano is too expensive, you could buy a keyboard. This is probably the most ⁵_____ instrument for small children.

Vocabulary

3 Order the words to make sentences.
   1 lots them of smoke can't stand with I restaurants in
   _____.
   2 eat he what mind we doesn't
   _____.
   3 food adore Italian absolutely I
   _____.
   4 keen food hot on I'm not too spicy
   _____.

4 Complete the sentences with a suitable word.
   1 The film is a m _ _ _ _ _ _ _ with lots of singing and dancing.
   2 It's a s _ _ _ _ _ _ _ f _ _ _ _ _ _ film about robots in space.
   3 It's a really funny film. It's the best c _ _ _ _ _ I've seen in my life.
   4 I've bought this DVD. It's a d _ _ _ _ about a woman whose husband disappears while he is working for the government.
   5 It's a f _ _ _ _ _ _ film with lots of magic and monsters.
   6 It's a r _ _ _ _ _ _ _ about a girl who meets the perfect man on holiday.

Pronunciation

5 Underline the word with different pronunciation of the –ed ending.
   1 bored   amazed   excited
   2 embarrassed   waited   shocked
   3 disgusted   stayed   interested
   4 played   fascinated   amazed

Check your answers on >> p.88

What are you going to do now?
   a Nothing. I'm happy.
   b Revise grammar/vocabulary/pronunciation and try again.
   c Ask another student/my teacher for help.

To revise, go to:
Student's Book Review >> p.45   Grammar Bank >> p.139
Workbook >> pp.22–25   www.oup.com/elt/result

Reading

Read these texts again.
   Workbook >> p.26 exercise 1
   Workbook >> p.27 exercise 7

How confident are you?
I can understand …
   ☐ some words
   ☐ with help
   ☐ when I read again
   ☐ everything

Listening

Listen to this audio again.
   Workbook >> p.26 audio script **4S.1**

How confident are you?
I can understand …
   ☐ some words
   ☐ with help
   ☐ when I listen again
   ☐ everything

Writing

Do this writing exercise again.
   Workbook >> p.27 exercise 12

How confident are you?
I can write …
   ☐ with help
   ☐ on my own
   ☐ with some mistakes
   ☐ with no mistakes

What are you going to do now?
   a Nothing. I'm happy.
   b Ask my teacher for help.
   c Practise my reading/listening/writing.

To practise go to …
Student's Book >> pp.36–44
Workbook >> pp.26–27
MultiROM Listening section
www.oup.com/elt/result

Unit 5 Self check

Grammar

1 Underline the correct words to complete the sentences.
 1 The man murdered/was murdered the victim with a knife.
 2 A plane has hijacked/has been hijacked!
 3 My bicycle stole/was stolen by a thief outside the supermarket!
 4 The earrings found/were found by a tree.
 5 There was a train crash yesterday but fortunately, nobody killed/was killed.

2 Complete the text with these verbs. Use the past perfect.

 be escape leave take

 I was walking back to the hotel when I noticed someone was following me. I ¹_____ to a concert and I ²_____ a taxi back to the hotel. The taxi couldn't take me to the door of the hotel so I had to walk the last 500 metres. I didn't stop till I reached the hotel. There I was safe. I ³_____ my attacker! However, my attacker followed me to the hotel. But he wasn't a robber and he hadn't been trying to attack me. He was the taxi driver and he was returning my bag. I ⁴_____ it in the taxi!

Vocabulary

3 Complete the sentences with a suitable word.
 1 The head of state of the USA is the p _ _ _ _ _ _ _ _ _ .
 2 France is a r _ _ _ _ _ _ _ _ because it doesn't have a royal family.
 3 We have e _ _ _ _ _ _ _ _ _ every five years to choose the members of parliament.
 4 The c _ _ _ _ _ _ _ of Germany is Berlin.
 5 There are three main p _ _ _ _ _ _ _ _ parties in the United Kingdom.

4 Correct the sentences. The mistake is underlined.
 1 It's <u>forbid</u> to walk on the grass.
 2 Riding bicycles is <u>permit</u>.
 3 Dogs aren't <u>allow</u> in this building.
 4 Feeding the animals is <u>prohibit</u>.

Pronunciation

5 Complete the table with these words. Decide whether the words in brackets should say *nouns* or *verbs*.

 ~~answer~~ ~~become~~ body complete confess murder protect

●● (_____)	●● (_____)
answer	become

Check your answers on >> p.88

What are you going to do now?
 a Nothing. I'm happy.
 b Revise grammar/vocabulary/pronunciation and try again.
 c Ask another student/my teacher for help.

To revise, go to:
Student's Book Review >> p.55 Grammar Bank >> p.140
Workbook >> pp.28–31 www.oup.com/elt/result

Reading

Read these texts again.
 Workbook >> p.32 exercise 1
 Workbook >> p.33 exercise 8

How confident are you?
I can understand …
 ☐ some words
 ☐ with help
 ☐ when I read again
 ☐ everything

Listening

Listen to this audio again.
 Workbook >> p.32 audio script 5S.1

How confident are you?
I can understand …
 ☐ some words
 ☐ with help
 ☐ when I listen again
 ☐ everything

Writing

Do this writing exercise again.
 Workbook >> p.33 exercise 13

How confident are you?
I can write …
 ☐ with help
 ☐ on my own
 ☐ with some mistakes
 ☐ with no mistakes

What are you going to do now?
 a Nothing. I'm happy.
 b Ask my teacher for help.
 c Practise my reading/listening/writing.

To practise go to …
Student's Book >> pp.46–54
Workbook >> pp.32–33
MultiROM Listening section
www.oup.com/elt/result

Unit 6 Self check

Grammar

1 Complete the sentences with *so* or *such*.
1. It's _____ a strange coincidence!
2. It's _____ wonderful to see you again!
3. I was _____ a fool to leave you!
4. You always were _____ a terrible driver!
5. I'm just _____ happy I've found you again!

2 Underline the correct words.
I dropped my wallet on the pavement after ¹leaving/to leave a café. When I noticed, it was too late ²returning/to return to the place and look for it. I phoned the bank to cancel my credit cards before going to bed. The next day, a man came to my house and returned my wallet to me. I thanked him for ³bringing/to bring it back and offered him €20 for ⁴helping/to help me. He refused the money and left. It's nice ⁵knowing/to know that there are people honest and friendly enough ⁶doing/to do something like this!

Vocabulary

3 Complete the sentences with a suitable word.
1. Al's really n ___ ___. He always wants to know what you are doing.
2. In English, it's p ___ ___ ___ ___ ___ to use 'please' and 'thank you' a lot.
3. I can't sleep at night because the neighbours are so n ___ ___ ___ ___.
4. My boss is really f ___ ___ ___ ___ ___ ___ ___. He always says 'hello' to me and chats to me in the morning.
5. Their children are never naughty. They are always w ___ ___ -___ ___ ___ ___ ___ ___ ___ ___.

4 Tick ✓ the correct sentence.
1. ☐ a I said that I had a deal to offer him.
   ☐ b I told that I had a deal to offer him.
2. ☐ a I said him to give me the money.
   ☐ b I told him to give me the money.
3. ☐ a He said the man that he was an estate agent.
   ☐ b He told the man that he was an estate agent.
4. ☐ a I said, 'We'll both be rich!'
   ☐ b I told, 'We'll both be rich!'

Pronunciation

5 Tick ✓ the words where the letters *gh* are pronounced as a vowel sound.
1. ☐ daughter   4. ☐ naughty
2. ☐ enough   5. ☐ neighbour
3. ☐ fight   6. ☐ rough

Check your answers on >> p.89

What are you going to do now?
a Nothing. I'm happy.
b Revise grammar/vocabulary/pronunciation and try again.
c Ask another student/my teacher for help.

To revise, go to:
Student's Book Review >> p.65   Grammar Bank >> p.141
Workbook >> pp.34–37   www.oup.com/elt/result

Reading

Read these texts again.
   Workbook >> p.38 exercise 1
   Workbook >> p.39 exercise 7

How confident are you?
I can understand …
   ☐ some words
   ☐ with help
   ☐ when I read again
   ☐ everything

Listening

Listen to this audio again.
   Workbook >> p.38 audio script **6S.1**

How confident are you?
I can understand …
   ☐ some words
   ☐ with help
   ☐ when I listen again
   ☐ everything

Writing

Do this writing exercise again.
   Workbook >> p.39 exercise 13

How confident are you?
I can write …
   ☐ with help
   ☐ on my own
   ☐ with some mistakes
   ☐ with no mistakes

What are you going to do now?
a Nothing. I'm happy.
b Ask my teacher for help.
c Practise my reading/listening/writing.

To practise go to …
Student's Book >> pp.56–64
Workbook >> pp.38–39
MultiROM Listening section
www.oup.com/elt/result

Unit 7 Self check

Grammar

1 Put the words in brackets in the correct place.
   1 Bienvenu Mouzieto knows he likes. (what)
   2 The Sapeurs know to show off their clothes. (how)
   3 'You are you wear.' (what)
   4 The Sapeurs know colours look good together. (which)
   5 Only the person who lent the clothes knows they came from. (where)

2 Tick ✓ or correct the sentences. Sometimes two answers are possible.
   1 ☐ It must be a man's room because there are men's clothes hanging behind the bed.
   2 ☐ He likes pictures so he might be an artist.
   3 ☐ He can have a lot of money because there's nothing in his house.
   4 ☐ She's wearing a wedding ring so she can't be married.
   5 ☐ She speaks with an Australian accent so she must be from England.

Vocabulary

3 Complete the sentences with these words.

   bald   ginger   clean   wavy   freckles

   1 He doesn't have a beard or a moustache. He's _____-shaven.
   2 If I go out in the sun, I get lots of _____ on my face.
   3 Peter's got _____ hair, not straight hair.
   4 Another word for red hair is _____ hair.
   5 What was the name of the man with the _____ head?

4 Complete the sentences with a suitable word.
   1 You use a c_____ to tidy your hair.
   2 A l_____ is another word for an arm or a leg.
   3 Your e_____ is the middle part of your arm, between your shoulder and your hand.
   4 You can go to a g_____ to do exercise.
   5 You have five t_____ on your foot.

Pronunciation

5 Underline the silent letters in each word.
   1 climb
   2 knee
   3 walking
   4 half
   5 knife
   6 thumb

Check your answers on >> p.89

What are you going to do now?
   a Nothing. I'm happy.
   b Revise grammar/vocabulary/pronunciation and try again.
   c Ask another student/my teacher for help.

To revise, go to …

Student's Book Review >> p.75   Grammar Bank >> p.142
Workbook >> pp.40–43   www.oup.com/elt/result

Reading

Read these texts again.
   Workbook >> p.44 exercise 2
   Workbook >> p.45 exercise 8

How confident are you?
I can understand …
   ☐ some words
   ☐ with help
   ☐ when I read again
   ☐ everything

Listening

Listen to this audio again.
   Workbook >> p.44 audio script 7S.1▶

How confident are you?
I can understand …
   ☐ some words
   ☐ with help
   ☐ when I listen again
   ☐ everything

Writing

Do this writing exercise again.
   Workbook >> p.45 exercise 13

How confident are you?
I can write …
   ☐ with help
   ☐ on my own
   ☐ with some mistakes
   ☐ with no mistakes

What are you going to do now?
   a Nothing. I'm happy.
   b Ask my teacher for help.
   c Practise my reading/listening/writing.

To practise go to …

Student's Book >> pp.66–74
Workbook >> pp.44–45
MultiROM Listening section
www.oup.com/elt/result

Unit 8 Self check

Grammar

1 Match the beginnings and endings of the sentences.
   1 When I was a child
   2 I lost my keys this morning but
   3 My cat's very clever. I think
   4 In the future we will
   5 Dr Irene Pepperberg's
   6 Millions of viewers were amazed to see

   a I could sing very well.
   b been able to show that parrots can actually think.
   c be able to communicate with dolphins.
   d how Rico could understand his owner's instructions.
   e she can understand me.
   f I was able to open the door with a credit card.

2 Tick ✓ the correct sentence.
   1 a ☐ I asked him where was he from.
     b ☐ I asked him where he was from.
   2 a ☐ They wanted to know where I lived.
     b ☐ They wanted to know where did I live.
   3 a ☐ He asked her how she does get to work.
     b ☐ He asked her how she gets to work.
   4 a ☐ She asked me what thought I of the news.
     b ☐ She asked me what I thought of the news.

Vocabulary

3 Underline the correct words to complete the text.
   Stephanie's car broke ¹down/up on the way to work, so she had to ring a garage for help. A recorded message said, 'I'm sorry, all our lines are busy. Please call ²out/back in five minutes'. When Stephanie called a second time, a secretary answered and said, 'Hold ³out/on, I'll put you through'. Then she got cut ⁴off/out again. Finally, she got ⁵through/by to a mechanic. He said he was busy and handed her over to a colleague.

4 Tick ✓ or correct the sentences.
   1 He asked me whether I spoke English.
   2 He promised post back the money to me when he got home.
   3 I agreed giving him the money.
   4 He refused taking the money.
   5 I warned the woman to give him anything.

Pronunciation

5 Underline the stressed syllable. The first one is done for you.
   1 ability   3 curiosity   5 reality
   2 activity   4 popularity   6 possibility

Check your answers on >> p.89

What are you going to do now?
   a Nothing. I'm happy.
   b Revise grammar/vocabulary/pronunciation and try again.
   c Ask another student/my teacher for help.

To revise, go to:
Student's Book Review >> p.85   Grammar Bank >> p.143
Workbook >> pp.46–49   www.oup.com/elt/result

Reading

Read these texts again.
   Workbook >> p.50 exercise 1
   Workbook >> p.51 exercise 6

How confident are you?
I can understand ...
   ☐ some words
   ☐ with help
   ☐ when I read again
   ☐ everything

Listening

Listen to this audio again.
   Workbook >> p.50 audio script **8S.1**

How confident are you?
I can understand ...
   ☐ some words
   ☐ with help
   ☐ when I listen again
   ☐ everything

Writing

Do this writing exercise again.
   Workbook >> p.51 exercise 13

How confident are you?
I can write ...
   ☐ with help
   ☐ on my own
   ☐ with some mistakes
   ☐ with no mistakes

What are you going to do now?
   a Nothing. I'm happy.
   b Ask my teacher for help.
   c Practise my reading/listening/writing.

To practise go to ...
Student's Book >> pp.76–84
Workbook >> pp.50–51
MultiROM Listening section
www.oup.com/elt/result

Unit 9 Self check

Grammar

1 Match the beginnings and endings of the sentences.
1 The days are getting shorter,
2 I guess we need it,
3 We don't want floods,
4 The nights aren't very long,
5 It's freezing out there,

a don't we?
b aren't they?
c isn't it?
d do we?
e are they?

2 Underline the correct words.
1 If you don't take your coat, you get / you'll get wet.
2 If he isn't / won't be careful, he'll hurt himself.
3 If it's foggy, you shouldn't / wouldn't drive fast.
4 What happens / would happen if we all had a personal helicopter?
5 If I would have / had more free time, I would learn the piano.

Vocabulary

3 Complete the text with a suitable word.
I'll need to work to maintain my body over the next five years. For example, I'll ¹p _ _ _ _ _ _ _ _ eat about 2,500 kilograms of food, I'll breathe about 40 million times and my heart will beat about 175 million times. The body never stops working and renewing itself. But it's not all good news. ²U _ _ _ _ _ _ _ _ _ _ _ _, some parts of my body won't get replaced. ³H _ _ _ _ _ _ _ _ _, I'll still have the same teeth in five years' time, because I ⁴d _ _ _ _ _ _ _ _ won't grow any new ones. And my brain will get lighter by one gram each year as a small part dies, never to be replaced.

4 Complete the sentences with these words.

phrase   desktop   faculty   alarm   room

1 I need the _____ clock to wake up in the morning.
2 The biology department is part of the science _____.
3 The hotel offers _____ service twenty-four hours a day.
4 When you go to Greece, do you want to borrow my Greek _____ book?
5 Do you prefer to use your _____ computer or your laptop?

Pronunciation

5 Underline the stressed words in these sentences.
1 My body will have changed.
2 I'll have found a job.
3 My fingernails will have grown.
4 I'll have bought my own place.

Check your answers on >> p.89

What are you going to do now?
a Nothing. I'm happy.
b Revise grammar/vocabulary/pronunciation and try again.
c Ask another student/my teacher for help.

To revise, go to:
Student's Book Review >> p.95   Grammar Bank >> p.144
Workbook >> pp.52–55   www.oup.com/elt/result

Reading

Read these texts again.
Workbook >> p.56 exercise 1
Workbook >> p.57 exercise 7

How confident are you?
I can understand …
☐ some words
☐ with help
☐ when I read again
☐ everything

Listening

Listen to this audio again.
Workbook >> p.56 audio script **9S.1**

How confident are you?
I can understand …
☐ some words
☐ with help
☐ when I listen again
☐ everything

Writing

Do this writing exercise again.
Workbook >> p.57 exercise 11

How confident are you?
I can write …
☐ with help
☐ on my own
☐ with some mistakes
☐ with no mistakes

What are you going to do now?
a Nothing. I'm happy.
b Ask my teacher for help.
c Practise my reading/listening/writing.

To practise go to …
Student's Book >> pp.86–94
Workbook >> pp.56–57
MultiROM Listening section
www.oup.com/elt/result

Unit 10 Self check

Grammar

1 Underline the correct words to complete the text.

The people on ¹the/a High Street all know each other. Everybody knows who ²the/a butcher is and who ³the/a greengrocer is. But there are some strange people and vehicles in town – ⁴the/an engineer, ⁵the/a lorry and ⁶the/a bulldozer. Nobody knows what they're doing here. But finally, everybody discovers the truth: they're building ⁷the/a new shopping mall.

2 Tick ✓ or correct the sentences.
1 ☐ They'll replace the camera as long you show the receipt.
2 ☐ I won't buy a jacket unless I need one.
3 ☐ I don't go to see the film until I've read the reviews.
4 ☐ I'll buy it as longer as there's a guarantee.
5 ☐ We'll leave as soon as Eric phones.

Vocabulary

3 Complete the sentences with suitable words.
1 There's only one p_____ of yogurt in the fridge.
2 I was really hungry and I ate a whole p_____ of biscuits.
3 Sorry, there's glass on the floor because I broke a j_____ of marmalade.
4 We need to buy soap, shampoo and a t_____ of toothpaste.
5 The t_____ of margarine is open. Where's the lid?

4 Complete the sentences with these words.

so   lately   almost   less   since

1 I've been working here for ten months, more or _____.
2 I bought this computer _____ three years ago.
3 I've been really busy _____, which means I haven't been going to the gym much.
4 I've been doing my homework for 15 minutes or _____.
5 I've been waiting here _____ 4 o'clock!

Pronunciation

5 Say the phrases aloud and match the phrases to the stress pattern.
1 Have you been waiting?   a •●•••●•
2 I've been sleeping.   b •●••●•
3 It hasn't been raining.   c ••●•

Check your answers on >> p.89

What are you going to do now?
a Nothing. I'm happy.
b Revise grammar/vocabulary/pronunciation and try again.
c Ask another student/my teacher for help.

To revise, go to:
Student's Book Review >> p.105   Grammar Bank >> p.145
Workbook >> pp.58–61   www.oup.com/elt/result

Reading

Read these texts again.
Workbook >> p.62 exercise 1
Workbook >> p.63 exercise 6

How confident are you?
I can understand …
☐ some words
☐ with help
☐ when I read again
☐ everything

Listening

Listen to this audio again.
Workbook >> p.62 audio script 10S.1

How confident are you?
I can understand …
☐ some words
☐ with help
☐ when I listen again
☐ everything

Writing

Do this writing exercise again.
Workbook >> p.63 exercise 11

How confident are you?
I can write …
☐ with help
☐ on my own
☐ with some mistakes
☐ with no mistakes

What are you going to do now?
a Nothing. I'm happy.
b Ask my teacher for help.
c Practise my reading/listening/writing.

To practise go to …
Student's Book >> pp.96–104
Workbook >> pp.62–63
MultiROM Listening section
www.oup.com/elt/result

Unit 11 Self check

Grammar

1 Complete the sentences with a suitable form of the verb in brackets.
 1 My parents are having their house _____. (decorate)
 2 He's going to have his meal _____ to his room. (bring)
 3 Is it possible to have my valuables _____ in the hotel safe, please? (put)
 4 You can have your hair _____ by a qualified hairdresser. (cut)
 5 I had three teeth _____ by the dentist. (take out)
 6 He had his car _____ by the hotel's driver. (park)

2 Tick ✓ the correct sentence.
 1 a ☐ It was in Edinburgh, where I was a student.
   b ☐ It was in Edinburgh, where was I a student.
 2 a ☐ I got petrol on my coat, which was new, and it was completely ruined.
   b ☐ I got petrol on my coat, that was new, and it was completely ruined.
 3 a ☐ It was worse for Duncan, whose car it was, because he never got it back.
   b ☐ It was worse for Duncan, who's car it was, because he never got it back.
 4 a ☐ I changed the tyre, what was flat.
   b ☐ I changed the tyre, which was flat.

Vocabulary

3 Complete the sentences with a suitable word.
 1 You can't drive a car here because it's a p _ _ _ _ _ _ _ _ _ street.
 2 The road ends in a T- j _ _ _ _ _ _ _ _. You have to turn left or right.
 3 The two roads meet at a c _ _ _ _ _ _ _ _ _.
 4 You can get a taxi at the taxi r _ _ _.
 5 This road doesn't go anywhere. It's a d _ _ _-e _ _ street.

4 Complete the sentences with these words.

vaccination   insurance   block   net   kit

 1 You need to take a mosquito _____ to protect yourself from malaria.
 2 You need to have a _____ certificate to show you have had an injection against typhoid.
 3 You should get medical _____ in case you are injured or have to go to hospital.
 4 You need to wear sun _____ to protect yourself from the sun.
 5 We're walking in the mountains without a guide so we've prepared our own first aid _____.

Pronunciation

5 <u>Underline</u> the word or phrase with the main stress in these questions.
 1 Will I need a travel guide?
 2 Are there any foods I should avoid?
 3 Did you show your passport?
 4 Should I take some sun block?

Check your answers on >> p.90

What are you going to do now?
 a Nothing. I'm happy.
 b Revise grammar/vocabulary/pronunciation and try again.
 c Ask another student/my teacher for help.

To revise, go to:
Student's Book Review >> p.115   Grammar Bank >> p.146
Workbook >> pp.64–67   www.oup.com/elt/result

Reading

Read these texts again.
 Workbook >> p.68 exercise 1
 Workbook >> p.69 exercise 9

How confident are you?
I can understand ...
 ☐ some words
 ☐ with help
 ☐ when I read again
 ☐ everything

Listening

Listen to this audio again.
 Workbook >> p.68 audio script **11S.1**

How confident are you?
I can understand ...
 ☐ some words
 ☐ with help
 ☐ when I listen again
 ☐ everything

Writing

Do this writing exercise again.
 Workbook >> p.69 exercise 15

How confident are you?
I can write ...
 ☐ with help
 ☐ on my own
 ☐ with some mistakes
 ☐ with no mistakes

What are you going to do now?
 a Nothing. I'm happy.
 b Ask my teacher for help.
 c Practise my reading/listening/writing.

To practise go to ...
Student's Book >> pp.106–114
Workbook >> pp.68–69
MultiROM Listening section
www.oup.com/elt/result

Unit 12 Self check

Grammar

1 Complete the sentences with *so*, *because*, or *in order to*.
   1 The woman was hungry _____ she hadn't eaten.
   2 She hadn't eaten _____ she was hungry.
   3 She went to the market _____ buy some food.
   4 We had a party _____ we'd passed all our exams.
   5 We invited our teacher to the party _____ say 'thank you' for helping us pass the exams.
   6 We asked everyone to bring some food to the party _____ there would be enough to eat.

2 <u>Underline</u> the correct words.
   1 If Monica had/would have told the police, they would have arrested her.
   2 If Fernando wouldn't have/hadn't shot a prisoner, the result would have been the same.
   3 If Basia hadn't realized the bag was hers, her daughter would have been/wouldn't be in big trouble.
   4 Neil wouldn't go/wouldn't have gone if Jim had asked him to stay.
   5 If the police wouldn't arrest/hadn't arrested an innocent man, Toni would have stayed silent.

Vocabulary

3 Tick ✓ or correct the sentences.
   1 ☐ I'm glad Suzie's coming to my birthday party.
   2 ☐ I wish I have a dog.
   3 ☐ I hope I never had another day like this in my life!
   4 ☐ I wish I can speak German.
   5 ☐ I one day hope I'll have a home of my own.

4 Complete the sentences with the correct word.
   1 A w_____ is a book or a film with cowboys and gun fights.
   2 A book where someone dies and the reader slowly learns how the crime happened is called a m_____ m_____.
   3 A h_____ is a frightening film with monsters, like *Dracula* or *Frankenstein*.
   4 A s_____ f_____ novel is about space or the future, often with aliens, robots and spaceships.

Pronunciation

5 <u>Underline</u> the stressed words in B's lines.
   1 A I wish I could speak Italian.
      B Really? I wish I could speak Spanish.
   2 A I wish I had a car.
      B Really? I just wish I could drive!

Check your answers on >> p.90
What are you going to do now?
   a Nothing. I'm happy.
   b Revise grammar/vocabulary/pronunciation and try again.
   c Ask another student/my teacher for help.

To revise, go to:
Student's Book Review >> p.125   Grammar Bank >> p.147
Workbook >> pp.70–73   www.oup.com/elt/result

Reading

Read these texts again.
   Workbook >> p.74 exercise 1
   Workbook >> p.75 exercise 7

How confident are you?
I can understand …
   ☐ some words
   ☐ with help
   ☐ when I read again
   ☐ everything

Listening

Listen to this audio again.
   Workbook >> p.74 audio script **12S.1**

How confident are you?
I can understand …
   ☐ some words
   ☐ with help
   ☐ when I listen again
   ☐ everything

Writing

Do this writing exercise again.
   Workbook >> p.75 exercise 14

How confident are you?
I can write …
   ☐ with help
   ☐ on my own
   ☐ with some mistakes
   ☐ with no mistakes

What are you going to do now?
   a Nothing. I'm happy.
   b Ask my teacher for help.
   c Practise my reading/listening/writing.

To practise go to …
Student's Book >> pp.116–124
Workbook >> pp.74–75
MultiROM Listening section
www.oup.com/elt/result

Self checks   87

Self checks answer key

Unit 1
Grammar
1 1 ✓
   2 He doesn't need help. He can do his homework by **himself**.
   3 Come on Rachel, let's introduce **ourselves** to the new teacher.
   4 Come to the party tonight. Don't stay at home by **yourself**.
   5 ✓
2 1 wants
   2 is holding
   3 are helping
   4 are talking
   5 like

Vocabulary
3 1 widower
   2 single
   3 niece
   4 divorced
   5 flatmate
   6 neighbour
4 1 pears
   2 flour
   3 weight
   4 flew
   5 rode
   6 threw

Pronunciation
5 1 X
   2 O
   3 K
   4 R
   5 I
   6 Q
   7 G

Unit 2
Grammar
1 1 Tourists **rarely** go to this area.
   2 They **hardly ever** go shopping.
   3 ✓
   4 They **quite often** miss Trafalgar Square.
   5 They **usually want** to see the sights.
2 1 b
   2 d
   3 c
   4 e
   5 a

Vocabulary
3 1 Central America
   2 the Middle East
   3 the South Pacific
   4 Muslim
   5 Christian
4 1 narrow
   2 leather
   3 handle
   4 float
   5 container

Pronunciation
5 1 /s/
   2 /k/
   3 /k/
   4 /g/
   5 /dʒ/
   6 /g/

Unit 3
Grammar
1 1 started
   2 didn't go
   3 has achieved
   4 fought
   5 has already learnt
2 1 I'm looking **after** my baby brother this afternoon.
   2 Don't worry about the dishes. I'll wash them **up** today.
   3 The story wasn't true. I made **it** up.
   4 Can you **turn** the music up? I can't hear it.
   5 The shoes were really uncomfortable so I took **them** off.

Vocabulary
3 1 blackboard
   2 history
   3 break
   4 teacher's pet
   5 canteen
4 1 professor
   2 lecturer
   3 Masters
   4 college
   5 classes

Pronunciation
5 ●●● beautiful, chemistry, colourful, happily
    ●●● achievement, successful
    ●●●● photography, technology
    ●●●● application, education

Unit 4
Grammar
1 1 b
   2 a
   3 b
2 1 cheaper
   2 convenient
   3 easily
   4 best
   5 popular

Vocabulary
3 1 I can't stand restaurants with lots of smoke in them.
   2 He doesn't mind what we eat.
   3 I absolutely adore Italian food.
   4 I'm not too keen on hot spicy food.
4 1 musical
   2 science fiction
   3 comedy
   4 drama
   5 fantasy
   6 romance

Pronunciation
5 1 excited
   2 shocked
   3 stayed
   4 fascinated

Unit 5
Grammar
1 1 murdered
   2 has been hijacked
   3 was stolen
   4 were found
   5 was killed
2 1 had been
   2 had taken
   3 had escaped
   4 had left

Vocabulary
3 1 president
   2 republic
   3 elections
   4 capital
   5 political
4 1 forbidden
   2 permitted
   3 allowed
   4 prohibited

Pronunciation
5 ●● (nouns) answer, body, murder
   ●● (verbs) become, complete, confess, protect

88 Self checks answer key

Unit 6
Grammar
1
1. such
2. so
3. such
4. such
5. so

2
1. leaving
2. to return
3. bringing
4. helping
5. to know
6. to do

Vocabulary
3
1. nosy
2. polite
3. noisy
4. friendly
5. well-behaved

4
1. a
2. b
3. b
4. a

Pronunciation
5
1. ✓
2.
3. ✓
4. ✓
5. ✓
6.

Unit 7
Grammar
1
1. Bienvenu Mouzieto knows **what** he likes.
2. The Sapeurs know **how** to show off their clothes.
3. 'You are **what** you wear.'
4. The Sapeurs know **which** colours look good together.
5. Only the person who lent the clothes knows **where** they came from.

2
1. ✓
2. ✓
3. He **can't** have a lot of money because there's nothing in his house.
4. She's wearing a wedding ring so she **must/might** be married.
5. She speaks with an Australian accent so she **can't** be from England.

Vocabulary
3
1. clean
2. freckles
3. wavy
4. ginger
5. bald

4
1. comb
2. limb
3. elbow
4. gym
5. toes

Pronunciation
5
1. clim<u>b</u>
2. <u>k</u>nee
3. wa<u>l</u>king
4. ha<u>l</u>f
5. <u>k</u>nife
6. thum<u>b</u>

Unit 8
Grammar
1
1. a
2. f
3. e
4. c
5. b
6. d

2
1. b
2. a
3. b
4. b

Vocabulary
3
1. down
2. back
3. on
4. off
5. through

4
1. ✓
2. He promised **to** post back the money to me when he got home.
3. I agreed **to give** him the money.
4. He refused **to take** the money.
5. I warned the woman **not** to give him anything.

Pronunciation
5
1. ab<u>i</u>lity
2. act<u>i</u>vity
3. cur<u>i</u>osity
4. popul<u>a</u>rity
5. re<u>a</u>lity
6. poss<u>i</u>bility

Unit 9
Grammar
1
1. b
2. a
3. d
4. e
5. c

2
1. you'll get
2. isn't
3. shouldn't
4. would happen
5. had

Vocabulary
3
1. probably
2. Unfortunately
3. Hopefully
4. definitely

4
1. alarm
2. faculty
3. room
4. phrase
5. desktop

Pronunciation
5
1. My <u>body</u> will have <u>changed</u>.
2. I'll have <u>found</u> a job.
3. My <u>fingernails</u> will have <u>grown</u>.
4. I'll have <u>bought</u> my <u>own</u> <u>place</u>.

Unit 10
Grammar
1
1. the
2. the
3. the
4. an
5. a
6. a
7. a

2
1. They'll replace the camera as long **as** you show the receipt.
2. ✓
3. I **won't** go to see the film until I've read the reviews.
4. I'll buy it as **long** as there's a guarantee.
5. ✓

Vocabulary
3
1. pot
2. packet
3. jar
4. tube
5. tub

4
1. less
2. almost
3. lately
4. so
5. since

Self checks answer key 89

Self checks answer key

Pronunciation
5 1 c
   2 b
   3 a

Unit 11

Grammar
1 1 decorated
   2 brought
   3 put
   4 cut
   5 taken out
   6 parked
2 1 a
   2 a
   3 a
   4 b

Vocabulary
3 1 pedestrian
   2 T-junction
   3 crossroads
   4 rank
   5 dead-end
4 1 net
   2 vaccination
   3 insurance
   4 block
   5 kit

Pronunciation
5 1 Will I need a <u>travel guide</u>?
   2 Are there any <u>foods</u> I should avoid?
   3 Did you show your <u>passport</u>?
   4 Should I take some <u>sun block</u>?

Vocabulary
3 1 ✓
   2 I wish I **had** a dog.
   3 I hope I never **have** another day like this in my life!
   4 I wish I **could** speak German.
   5 I **hope one day** I'll have a home of my own.
4 1 western
   2 murder mystery
   3 horror
   4 science fiction

Pronunciation
5 1 Really? <u>I</u> wish I could speak <u>Spanish</u>.
   2 Really? <u>I</u> just wish I could <u>drive</u>!

Unit 12

Grammar
1 1 because
   2 so
   3 in order to
   4 because
   5 in order to
   6 so
2 1 If Monica <u>had</u> told the police, they would have arrested her.
   2 If Fernando <u>hadn't</u> shot a prisoner, the result would have been the same.
   3 If Basia hadn't realized the bag was hers, her daughter <u>would have been</u> in big trouble.
   4 Neil <u>wouldn't have gone</u> if Jim had asked him to stay.
   5 If the police <u>hadn't arrested</u> an innocent man, Toni would have stayed silent.

90 Self checks answer key

Audio scripts

1

1B.1
1 That's Miss Wilson.
2 Here's Ms Wilson now.
3 This is Mr Wilson.
4 There's Mrs Wilson.
5 Hello, Miss Brady.
6 Goodbye Mrs Brady.
7 There's a letter for Ms Brady.
8 Good morning, Mr Brady.

1D.1
1 g
2 z
3 p
4 t
5 j
6 y
7 q
8 m
9 i
10 e

1D.2
1 j-o-k-e, joke
2 p-h-r-a-s-e-s, phrases
3 b-o-t-t-l-e-s, bottles
4 l-a-z-y, lazy
5 s-p-e-a-k, speak
6 c-o-m-p-l-e-t-e-d, completed
7 q-u-i-e-t-l-y, quietly
8 l-a-n-g-u-a-g-e, language

1S.1
1
A Hey, that's a lovely shirt you're wearing! Where did you get it?
B Skirt? What skirt? I'm not wearing a skirt!
A No, no! Not a skirt! Your shirt! S-**H**-I-R-T!
B Oh! Right! Er, sorry, I thought you said *skirt*.
A So, where did you get it?
B Ah, er, it was a present, actually.

2
A Anything else, madam?
B Yes, please. Um, half a kilo of peas.
A Of course. Blue or white?
B Blue or white?
A Yes, madam. We have a blue cheese, that's quite strong in flavour, and a white cheese. That's very fresh and mild. Which one would you like?
B But I asked you for peas. P-E-A-S. And peas are green!
A So ... you don't want any cheese?
B No, thank you! Just half a kilo of peas!
A Coming up, madam.

3
A Excuse me! Are you ready to order now?
B Yes, please. Fish for my wife.
A Which fish, sir? The salmon or the tuna?
B Er, the tuna, please. With rice.
A Right. And for you, sir?
B Well, what's the soap of the day?
A Soap, sir?
B Yes, what kind of soap do you have?
A Erm, the soap's in the toilet, sir. Do you mean soup? We have some delicious vegetable soup today ...
B Oh, yes, yes of course! Soup! I'm sorry.

4
A And your surname, please?
B Welsh.
A Could you just spell that?
B W – E – L – S - H
A W – E – L – S – 8. So why do you have a number at the end of your name?
B A number? What number? I don't have a number in my name!
A I thought you said L – S – 8?
B Oh goodness, no! L – S – **H**!
A Oh I see! Sorry!

2

2A.1
golden
city
region
games
typical
central
face
egg
place
together
marriage
costume
Atlantic
fact
bag
Germany

2B.1
She says she never goes
To the places that she knows.
But the food, she always tries
If the restaurant's won a prize.
And you can often see her queue
For tickets to somewhere new.
She rarely hires a car
The monuments aren't that far.

She usually takes the bus
Sits with locals just like us.
Quite often, she'll stop and chat
To find out where you're at.
Sometimes she even stops for tea
But she hardly ever writes to me!

2C.1
1 What's it used as?
2 It's from Germany.
3 It's used for opening letters.
4 What's it made of?
5 What's it used for?
6 It's used as an instrument.
7 Where's it from?
8 It's made of plastic.

2S.1
M Gerry Bayne! I haven't seen you for ages!
G Hello, Maggie! I thought you lived in Spain now?
M Oh, I'm just home for Christmas for a week or so.
G How's it all going?
M Well, pretty good on the whole ... but I still have problems adapting.
G Like what?
M Well, just the other day, for example. In Spain, when you meet people, you kiss them on the cheeks.
G And?
M Well, I met some new people, and when I went to kiss them on the cheeks, they kind of stood back.
G Oh yes?
M I felt very uncomfortable. But my friends say that not everyone kisses people on the cheeks, not even the Spanish themselves.
G So how do you know what to do?
M Well, they say it's best to wait just a moment, watch what the other person does, and then just do the same.
G Hmm. Well, I can think of a few cases when that doesn't work either.
M Really?
G Yes. I was working in Sri Lanka and southern India recently.
M Lucky you!
G Right ... but I was always getting confused because they shake their heads to say yes, and nod their heads to say no.
M I didn't know that!
G Yes, they do it all the time. Just the opposite of what we do. And I just couldn't get used to it.
M Well, they must find it difficult to understand what we mean, too.
G Yes, that's true. I didn't think of that.

3

3A.1
top of the class
took the bus
finally met
lunch break
childhood dreams
French class
teacher's pet

3D.1
1 electric
2 electricity
3 investigation
4 investigate
5 dentist
6 dentistry
7 criminal
8 criminology
9 photography
10 photograph

3S.1
1
I went to school in my home town, Hannover, in northern Germany. I lived near the school and cycled there and back every day. Yes, it was OK. I learned a lot, and then I went to university, to, um, study Chemistry. It was always my favourite subject at school. The Chemistry teacher was great fun and his lessons were always interesting. I didn't like Languages; they were so boring. But of course, I've had to learn English since I left school, for my professional life.

2
I come from a small town in central France. School? Er, I went away to boarding school because there was no high school in my town. So I ate and slept at school during the week, and stayed at home with my family at weekends. I didn't mind too much, but I missed my mother's cooking. The meals at school weren't very nice! The school subjects were not so difficult for me, but, er, I didn't like Chemistry very much – there were always terrible smells in the Chemistry lab!

3
I went to school in the south of Spain, and it was very traditional – the teacher was always right! If you didn't understand the explanations, you must be a bit stupid. Most of the subjects were boring for me. I had to repeat my exams in September quite a lot. Oh, but I enjoyed being with my classmates. And the basketball team I played in always did very well in competitions.

4
I have very mixed memories of school. I went to a secondary school in the north of England. We learned our subjects well enough, but when I look back on it, I don't think school prepared me for real life. Everyone said how important it was to get good marks, but nobody taught us how to make decisions. They still had corporal punishment, if we got into trouble. You know, the teachers were allowed to hit us on the hands with a cane. That doesn't happen any more

these days. Just as well, because it certainly didn't solve anyone's problems!

4

4A.1
stayed
embarrassed
waited
amazed
interested
annoyed
excited
relaxed
decided
fascinated
stopped

4B.1
1 a big venue
2 a bigger venue
3 a quieter song
4 a quiet song
5 a loud sound
6 a louder sound
7 a longer concert
8 a long concert
9 a heavy instrument
10 a heavier instrument
11 an old singer
12 an older singer

4C.1
1 **A** How about going out tonight?
   B That sounds good!
2 **A** Why don't we leave now?
   B I'm not sure that's a good idea.
3 **A** Let's go to the pub!
   B Erm, I'd prefer not to, if you don't mind.
4 **A** What about going away this weekend?
   B That's a great idea!
5 **A** How about a cup of coffee?
   B Er, no thanks. I'm not very keen on coffee.
6 **A** Why don't we order a takeaway?
   B Yes, I'd really like that!

4S.1
M Hey, Vanessa! How are you?
V Not bad, thanks, Max. And you?
M Fine today. Not so good yesterday, though.
V So what happened yesterday?
M You didn't go to the Skitsoid Kids' concert, did you?
V No, I couldn't get tickets! So what was it like?
M Well, the first part was pretty exciting. We were halfway down the stadium, but we could see the band on the big video screens.
V Did they play *Hate your Love*? That's my favourite song. I absolutely adore the guitar solo in the middle!
M Yeah, they did. Um, the rock songs were just amazing. But I'm not so keen on the slow songs, you know, the ballads.
V Don't you like them?
M I can't stand them. They're so boring.
V Oh – I think they do them

really well.
M Anyway, like I said, the first part was great, but the second part was really bad.
V Why? What happened?
M To begin with, we couldn't hear the vocals properly. That's really annoying. The sound quality was dreadful, and I couldn't hear the words.
V What a shame!
M Yes. But that wasn't the worst thing!
V You mean it got worse than that?
M Haven't you heard? They had to cancel the second part of the concert, because of the rain.
V Oh no! I didn't know that! That's terrible! I mean, you don't mind getting cold if the music's all right, but heavy rain is a different matter. You must be really disappointed, then.
M Yeah. They say they'll do another concert in the spring.
V Well, that's good news!
M Mmm. But I don't know if I'll go next time.
V Well, I'll make sure I get a ticket for that one!

5

5A.1
the British
the Americans
the UN
the president
the elections
the age of democracy
the government
the Austrian president
the Irish flag
the Republic of South Africa

5C.1
plane crash
cash machine
petrol station
murder victim
baseball bat
taxi driver
bus stop
bank robber
car key

5D.1
1 body
2 attack
3 column
4 reason
5 return
6 begin
7 neighbour
8 repeat
9 appear
10 building
11 picture
12 survive

5S.1
C Hi, John! Have you just come back from your summer break?
J Hi there, Cornelia! Yes, I got back home last weekend. Did you have a good summer?
C Great, thanks. I heard you've

been living and working in a kind of community!
J That's right. It was just incredible!
C So, tell me more! Where was it? What was it like?
J Well, I was in a village restoration project in Italy.
C A what?
J Well, it's voluntary, and it's a kind of work camp you do in the summer holidays. And the volunteers live and work together, and share experiences.
C Experiences?
J There are people from lots of different countries. We talked a lot, and exchanged stories about where we're from and things.
C So what did you actually do there?
J We lived in a primary school, we shared the kitchen and bathroom, but there were separate bedrooms. I shared a room with an American, a German, and a guy from Croatia.
C Hmm. A bit like a large family then?
J Yes, that describes it pretty well!
C So was it easy to get along together?
J Sometimes yes, sometimes no! But we didn't have any serious problems.
C And what kind of work did you have to do?
J Basically, we worked outside. There were a lot of plants in the village, so we cleared the streets and paths, and, um, we repaired fences and stone walls.
C Wow. But you didn't work seven days a week?
J Definitely not! Weekends were free. I mean, you have to have time to relax.
C Mmm. Would you recommend the experience?
J Absolutely! I made a lot of good friends. I learned a lot about Italy and also Croatia. Yeah, I had a great time!
C That sounds good! Can you give me an email address for more information?

6

6A.1
1 That's such dreadful news!
2 She has such fantastic ideas!
3 She's such a wonderful person!
4 This is so depressing!
5 It's such an amazing project!
6 His classes are just so boring!

6C.1
caught
enough
fight
night
daughter
naughty

rough
neighbour
eight
bought
high
laugh
cough

6D.1
She said he'd have to go
He said he didn't know
She said she needed a break
He said he'd made a mistake
They said they'd talked enough
They said they'd have to break up.

6S.1
A
A So, have you ever lost anything?
B Well, not exactly lost, no. But I once had my camera stolen.
A That's terrible! What happened?
B Er, I was travelling with friends and we stopped to have a meal, and I left the bag in the car.
A Hmm. A bit risky, though.
B I thought it was safe enough, because I could see the car from the restaurant.
A Aha! But the thieves got in anyway.
B Yeah, from the other side.
A Oh dear! Did you ever get it back?
B No way! But luckily it was insured, so I bought another one with the insurance money.
A Well that wasn't so bad then, was it?
B No, that was OK. Just that I lost all the photos. Anyway, what about you?

B
A Me? Oh, I think the worst thing I've ever lost was a couple of suitcases at an airport.
B Really?
A That's right. We'd been to South Africa, on holiday, and then flew back home.
B A direct flight?
A No, it wasn't. We stopped for a few hours in Nigeria. But that wasn't the problem.
B Uh-huh …
A Well, the suitcases just didn't appear in the airport. They couldn't find them anywhere.
B Didn't you get them back later?
A Oh, we filled in a lot of forms, and made a lot of phone calls, but we never saw them again.
B Oh. And what was in the cases?
A Mainly clothes and stuff, you know. But what really hurt was losing all the presents we'd bought for the family. There was no way the airline could replace them.
B What a shame!
A Yeah. The only thing the family got to see was the photos, because we had the camera in our hand luggage.

C
A Well I lost my car once, you know.
B Your car? How could you

possibly lose your car?
A But I did, I'm telling you! I had to go up to Scotland on a business trip for a week, you see, so I took the car.
B And?
A Well, it was that time of year. I mean, it was late January – the middle of winter.
B Did somebody steal the car?
A No, no! There was a freak snowstorm during the night, and when I came down in the morning, I couldn't see the car park for the snow!
B And the cars?
A All buried in the snow!
B Did you have to dig it out, then?
A Oh, no! They told us we'd have to wait a day or two for the snow to melt, otherwise we'd only damage the cars.
B So what did you do?
A I just stayed an extra couple of days in the hotel! The roads were all blocked anyway ...

7

7A.1
1 **A** Has he got long fair hair?
   B No, short fair hair.
2 **A** Has he got short curly hair?
   B No, short dark hair.
3 **A** Has she got big dark eyes?
   B No, small dark eyes.
4 **A** Has she got small brown eyes?
   B No, small blue eyes.
5 **A** Has he got a bald head?
   B No, a shaved head.

7B.1
1 I don't care what I wear.
2 I can't imagine why you bought that.
3 Your outfit looks lovely.
4 Where did you get that dress?

7C.1
time	climb
home	comb
arm	calm
drum	thumb
life	knife
sea	knee
fork	walk
so	know
laugh	half

7S.1
A
I don't really know what I want to do when I leave school. I think I'll probably take a year off, maybe go abroad and find a job. I speak a bit of Spanish, so I could go to Spain. I like the sound of the Canary Islands! Lots of sunshine all year. And then after that? Well, I suppose I'll start looking for a proper job. My uncle's got two shops in town, and I could help him there. And when I get enough money, I'm going to buy a car!
B
When I finish my degree, the first thing I'm going to do is find a Mediterranean beach and do nothing for two weeks! After that, I'm going to travel around Mexico for a month. I've got a friend who works there, and I've always wanted to visit that part of the world. Then it'll be time to start work. I've had five interviews in the last four months, and one of them offered me a job, so I may start with them and see what happens. That'll be in September.
C
Summer holidays? I haven't thought about them, really. Haven't had much time. We're a bit tired of the beach, so we'll probably go for something different this year. Maybe a touring holiday with a caravan. You know, go and see France properly. Or maybe we'll rent one of those mountain chalets in Switzerland and enjoy the fresh air. But I mean, we're definitely going abroad. The weather's always better!
D
The Christmas holidays? Well, we can't really go abroad, because there isn't enough time. The children are still at school till the week before Christmas. We usually go to my parents' house on Christmas Day, and for New Year's Day we go to my husband's parents. I imagine we'll probably do the same this year – it'll be good to spend some time with them. One thing we're not going to do is leave all the shopping till the last minute. I've done most of the shopping already and we're going out on Friday for the final few presents.

8

8B.1
able
curiosity
popularity
possible
reality
electric
responsible
quality
opportunity
quantity

8D.1
He asked me not to pack
I told him not to wait
He asked me to call him back
I told him it was just too late
He told me I'd be sorry
I told him not to worry
And left him by the gate

8S.1
A You know Saskia who works in the clothes shop?
B Yeah?
A Well, the most incredible thing happened to her last week.
B Oh yeah? What was that?
A Well, there she was, organizing the clothes in the shop, when this man came in.
B And?
A He said he wanted a dress for his wife's birthday. So, Saskia asked him about all the usual things – size, colour .... and she showed him what they had in the shop.
B Mmm ...
A He looked through them, chose two, and paid for them in cash. But ten minutes later, he came back again.
B Why was that?
A He said one of the dresses was too small, and asked Saskia to find a bigger size for him. So she went into the back of the shop to find one, but when she came out, he was gone.
B Well maybe he was in a hurry.
A Well, yes, I suppose he was! Because he took the shop computer and cash till as well!
B You're joking!
A No, no! It's all true!
B But how did he manage that? I mean, cash machines are big, heavy things! You don't carry them around in a shopping bag!
A Well, it seems he parked a small van just outside the shop, left the van open, put the machines in the back and just drove off. It happened so fast that nobody really noticed! People only realized there was something wrong when Saskia came running out of the shop!

9

9A.1
1 It's strange weather today, isn't it?
2 Those clouds don't look very good, do they?
3 It looks like rain over there, doesn't it?
4 The rain never lasts long though, does it?
5 It'll rain later, won't it?
6 It isn't very cold, is it?
7 You've got a real passion for weather, haven't you?
8 You haven't noticed I'm trying to read, have you?

9B.1
1 My sister will have left school.
   (My sister'll've left school.)
2 My father will have stopped working.
   (My father'll've stopped working.)
3 I'll have finished my degree.
   (I'll've finished my degree.)
4 My sister won't have got married.
   (My sister won't've got married.)
5 My brother won't have left home.
   (My brother won't've left home.)
6 I won't have bought a flat.
   (I won't've bought a flat.)

9D.1
Where did you go, why did you go?
Who did you see, what did you see?
Why did you not tell me?
How would you know, when would you know?
Who would you choose, which would you choose?
When would you let me go?

9S.1
S Hey guys! My grandfather left me some money in his will, and I'm thinking of giving it to charity. What do you think?
Do Great idea! Good for you, Stella. How about *Green Planet*? They do lots of great environmental work all over the world.
S Yes, I suppose so. I don't know much about them though, Donna.
Do Well, if you give them the money, it'll go directly into green projects, like protecting the rainforests, or helping endangered animals.
Dm Hang on a minute! They also spend a lot of money on political campaigning, don't they?
Do But only where governments are doing things to harm the environment.
Dm OK, but if I had money to give to charity, I'd want to be sure I knew where that money is going.
S Maybe you've got a point, Dmitri. So what would you suggest instead?
Dm I'd give money to charities for people, before the environment. How about that *OrfanCare* charity we saw the advert for? That has to be a good cause, doesn't it? Orphans in Africa?
S That's true. But without a better environment, we're all going to die anyway!
Do I'm with Stella. Quite right! Climate change will cause all sorts of natural disasters if we don't act quickly. *Green Planet* are campaigning for governments to use solar power and recycle their paper.
Dm What's that got to do with it? That's not going to change the world very quickly, is it?
S I think you might be right there, Dmitri. I want to support a charity that makes a real difference to real people.
Dm Exactly! Well, why not sponsor a child then? You can't get much more real-world than that. You get to know a real child and their family, and your money helps the whole community on development projects, schools, healthcare, that kind of thing.
S Really? That sounds perfect! Can you tell me more about it?

10

10B.1
1 six packets of crisps.
2 two bottles of mineral water.
3 three boxes of chocolates.
4 a can of lemonade.
5 four cartons of orange juice.
6 a jar of honey.
7 a tube of toothpaste.
8 four tins of pineapple.
9 two tubs of ice cream.
10 three bags of shopping.

10C.1
It's been raining
It hasn't been sunny
It's been freezing
It hasn't been funny
Have I been waiting?
I've been waiting for summer

10S.1
R Bill!
B Yes, dear?
R Where did all these mirrors come from?
B Erm, there was a clearance sale at the furniture shop, dear. Four for the price of three!
R But we don't need ten mirrors, Bill, do we?
B All right, but we can keep them for the children! You know, for when they're older!
R I don't think so, Bill. Our children are not yet four years old! And in any case, we haven't got enough walls for so many mirrors!
B Well, OK, I suppose you're right. But you must admit, those shoes were a real bargain!
R Which shoes? The ones you bought last week?
B No – the three pairs I bought this morning.
R Oh, no – you haven't been buying shoes again!
B Only three pairs!
R But you promised me you wouldn't buy any more!
B OK, that's true. But they're real leather, and the price was just unbeatable!
R Where did you get the money?
B I borrowed it from my sister. I'm going to pay it back.
R But she told me she wouldn't lend you any more – she must be crazy!
B Well, I'm not so sure about that. She was just helping her brother. She didn't even ask what the money was for.
R Bill, we've been having this shopping problem for three years now. Last year you spent all our holiday money. We had to cancel your credit card. We talked it all over, and you understood you had a problem. Now I discover you've been buying more stuff that we don't need. I thought things were getting better!
B Well, I'm not spending as much as I used to, Ruth. And somebody has to do the shopping!
R I know, but we agreed I'd do that until you got better.
B Well, maybe, but I just get bored if I can't go out.
R Look, Bill. This has gone too far. You'll have to choose: it's me or the shops.
B OK, OK. I suppose you're right. I'll call Barney and see if he wants to go out and play golf.

11

11C.1
1 Should I take any sun block with me?
2 Do we need to get some travel insurance?
3 Will there be accommodation for us?
4 Did you bring the road maps?
5 How good is public transport?
6 What kind of food should I avoid?

11D.1
1 She lives near the park where I used to play.
2 She lives near the park, where I used to play.
3 We asked the policeman, who was on the corner.
4 We asked the policeman who was on the corner.
5 I carried the suitcase which was heavy.
6 I carried the suitcase, which was heavy.

11S.1
A Hello! How are you?
B Not so bad, thanks. And you?
A Fine, fine. Listen, I wanted to ask you …
B What?
A Didn't you travel to South Asia a few years ago?
B Yeah, that's right. We visited parts of India and Sri Lanka. Why?
A I wanted to ask you about health stuff, you know, injections before you go, the 'dos' and 'don'ts' while you're there.
B Oh right. Let me just think. Ah yes, we got several vaccinations before we left. I think the three most important are hepatitis, cholera and typhoid.
A What about malaria?
B Well, for malaria you need to take anti-malaria pills, and a good mosquito net!
A OK. Is there anything else I should know?
B Probably the most important thing is that you ought to drink only boiled water.
A Boiled water? Isn't bottled water all right?
B You can't really be sure. Boiled is best. Ah, and no ice.
A Ice?
B Yeah, you know, in drinks and things. You shouldn't have ice.
A Because you don't know if it's from boiled water, right?
B Right! And never eat in the street. I mean, find a proper restaurant for your meals.
A OK. That sounds reasonable.
B And in any case, take out medical insurance before you travel. Just in case.
A Oh, I hadn't thought of that! A very sensible thing to do, huh?
B Absolutely!
A Thanks a lot. That's very helpful!
B No trouble! Have a good trip!

12

12A.1
1 I think Bat was very stupid.
2 I think the birds were too jealous.
3 It's just like those Aesop stories.
4 I think the moral is that everyone should know their place.

12B.1
1 **A** I wish I had a car like yours!
   B Really? I wish I had a boyfriend like yours!
2 **A** I wish I didn't work in a shop!
   B Really? I just wish I had a job!
3 **A** I hope it doesn't rain tomorrow!
   B Really? I hope it does rain – I don't want to go out!
4 **A** I'm glad he's leaving the company!
   B Really? I wish he was staying!

12C.1
A Well, as I was saying, it's a kind of science-fiction story, and it takes place on this strange planet. Anyway, there's a group of survivors who …
B Well, I suppose this is a horror story. It starts off with these dead bodies in a car. Anyway, the hero and his girlfriend have to escape …

12D.1
I would have waited if you'd asked.
I would have called if you'd waited.
I would have written if you'd replied.
But you wouldn't have asked.
You wouldn't have waited.
And you wouldn't have replied.
So now you know why
I didn't wait or call or write.

12S.1
1 Caroline
Well, I studied biology at university. But when I graduated, I didn't like the jobs that were on offer – I didn't want to work in a big company, and I knew that I didn't want to teach either. So I went abroad to do voluntary work in Namibia. It was very difficult to begin with. I mean, the climate was totally different, living conditions weren't the same. We often didn't have water for two or three days. But, in time, I grew to love the place, and especially the people. Nowadays, I live and work for six months in the UK, and the other six months in Namibia. I have the best of both worlds! Going abroad was probably the most important decision I've ever made.

2 Jeff
Erm, I remember I was 28 at the time, and I'd had the same job for about six years. I designed video games. I mean, the computer part of the games. It was interesting enough, but I needed to do something with my hands. So I signed up for a three-month part-time painting course. And then I met this woman on the course. I mean, I just went crazy. Couldn't take my eyes off her – and she noticed. Well, we started going out together. And that was a big scandal at home, because she was ten years older than me. Just think of it: if I hadn't done the course, I'd never have met her. We've been together for nearly fifteen years, now.

3 Lizzy
I was a terrible student at school. You know, just couldn't get interested in anything. The teachers were boring, the subjects didn't mean anything to me. So of course I got bad marks and then had problems at home – the usual kind of reactions. And then halfway through the third year, this new English teacher arrived, and we started reading these books that just became alive. I don't know how to explain it, but this guy asked questions that no-one else had ever done, and wanted to know our opinions about what we were reading. I failed most of my exams, but because of him, I started writing on my own. I'm 35 now, and I've had six novels published. If he hadn't appeared at school, I'd probably have left at sixteen and gone to work in a fast-food restaurant!

Irregular verbs

verb	past simple	past participle
be	was	been
	were	
become	became	become
begin	began	begun
bite	bit	bitten /ˈbɪtn/
blow	blew	blown
break	broke	broken
bring	brought /brɔːt/	brought /brɔːt/
build /bɪld/	built /bɪlt/	built /bɪlt/
burn	burnt	burnt
	burned	burned
buy	bought /bɔːt/	bought /bɔːt/
catch	caught /kɔːt/	caught /kɔːt/
choose	chose /tʃəʊz/	chosen /ˈtʃəʊzn/
come	came	come
cost	cost	cost
cut	cut	cut
do	did	done
draw	drew	drawn
dream	dreamt /dremt/	dreamt /dremt/
	dreamed	dreamed
drink	drank	drunk
drive	drove	driven /ˈdrɪvn/
eat	ate	eaten
fall	fell	fallen
feel	felt	felt
find	found	found
fly	flew	flown
forget	forgot	forgotten
forgive	forgave	forgiven /fəˈgɪvn/
freeze	froze	frozen
get	got	got
give	gave	given
go	went	gone
		been
grow	grew	grown
hang	hung	hung
have	had	had
hear	heard /hɜːd/	heard /hɜːd/
hide	hid	hidden /ˈhɪdn/
hit	hit	hit
hold	held	held

verb	past simple	past participle
hurt	hurt	hurt
keep	kept	kept
know	knew /njuː/	known /nəʊn/
learn	learnt	learnt
	learned	learned
leave	left	left
lend	lent	lent
let	let	let
lie	lay	lain
lose	lost	lost
make	made	made
mean	meant /ment/	meant /ment/
meet	met	met
mistake	mistook /mɪˈstʊk/	mistaken
pay	paid	paid
put	put	put
read	read /red/	read /red/
ride	rode	ridden /ˈrɪdn/
ring	rang	rung
rise	rose	risen /ˈrɪzn/
run	ran	run
say	said /sed/	said /sed/
see	saw /sɔː/	seen
sell	sold	sold
send	sent	sent
set	set	set
shake	shook /ʃʊk/	shaken
shine	shone /ʃɒn/	shone /ʃɒn/
show	showed	shown
shut	shut	shut
sing	sang	sung
sink	sank	sunk
sit	sat	sat
sleep	slept	slept
smell	smelt	smelt
	smelled	smelled
speak	spoke	spoken
spell	spelt	spelt
	spelled	spelled
spend	spent	spent
split	split	split

verb	past simple	past participle
spoil	spoilt	spoilt
stand	stood /stʊd/	stood /stʊd/
steal	stole	stolen
stick	stuck	stuck
swear	swore	sworn
swim	swam	swum
take	took /tʊk/	taken
teach	taught /tɔːt/	taught /tɔːt/
tear	tore	torn
tell	told	told
think	thought /θɔːt/	thought /θɔːt/
throw	threw	thrown
understand	understood	understood
wake up	woke up	woken up
wear	wore	worn
win	won /wʌn/	won /wʌn/
write	wrote	written /ˈrɪtn/

« Look at the verb column. Cover the past simple and past participle columns and test yourself.

OXFORD
UNIVERSITY PRESS

Great Clarendon Street, Oxford OX2 6DP

Oxford University Press is a department of the University of Oxford.
It furthers the University's objective of excellence in research, scholarship,
and education by publishing worldwide in

Oxford New York

Auckland Cape Town Dar es Salaam Hong Kong Karachi
Kuala Lumpur Madrid Melbourne Mexico City Nairobi
New Delhi Shanghai Taipei Toronto

With offices in

Argentina Austria Brazil Chile Czech Republic France Greece
Guatemala Hungary Italy Japan Poland Portugal Singapore
South Korea Switzerland Thailand Turkey Ukraine Vietnam

OXFORD and OXFORD ENGLISH are registered trade marks of
Oxford University Press in the UK and in certain other countries

© Oxford University Press 2009

The moral rights of the author have been asserted

Database right Oxford University Press (maker)

First published 2009

2013 2012 2011 2010
10 9 8 7 6

All rights reserved. No part of this publication may be reproduced,
stored in a retrieval system, or transmitted, in any form or by any means,
without the prior permission in writing of Oxford University Press (with
the sole exception of photocopying carried out under the conditions stated
in the paragraph headed 'Photocopying'), or as expressly permitted by law, or
under terms agreed with the appropriate reprographics rights organization.
Enquiries concerning reproduction outside the scope of the above should
be sent to the ELT Rights Department, Oxford University Press, at the
address above

You must not circulate this book in any other binding or cover
and you must impose this same condition on any acquirer

Photocopying

The Publisher grants permission for the photocopying of those pages marked
'photocopiable' according to the following conditions. Individual purchasers
may make copies for their own use or for use by classes that they teach.
School purchasers may make copies for use by staff and students, but this
permission does not extend to additional schools or branches

Under no circumstances may any part of this book be photocopied for resale

Any websites referred to in this publication are in the public domain and
their addresses are provided by Oxford University Press for information only.
Oxford University Press disclaims any responsibility for the content

ISBN: 978 0 19 430488 7

Printed in Spain by Orymu, S.A.

This book is printed on paper from certified and well-managed sources.

ACKNOWLEDGEMENTS

Illustrations by: David Atkinson/Handmade Maps pp10, 64; Emma Brownjohn/New Division pp5, 54; Gill Button p49; Mark Duffin: pp29 (signs), 43; Laure Fournier/The Organisation, 69; Simon Gurr pp11, 13, 40, 41, 50, 67, 71; Andy Hammond/Illustration pp8, 12, 66, 73; Joanna Kerr pp7, 23, 29; Gavin Reece pp6, 20, 31, 36, 52; Susan Scott p18; Alastair Taylor p63.

The Publishers and Authors would also like to thank the following for kind permission to reproduce photographs: Alamy Images pp14 (Long Neck Karen Hilltribe/Jon Arnold Images Ltd), 15 (The Elephanta Caves/Tom Hanley), 17 (Main Street Breckenridge Colorado/Ian Dagnall), 22 (Mexican milk snake/Bill Draker/Rolfnp), 26 (music festival fans/Jack Carey), 32 (Cow/imagebroker), 32 (pensioner in Bethnal Green/Kathy deWitt), 32 (Apartment block/imagebroker), 38 (playground/Caro), 38 (Detached house/Paul Thompson Images), 39 (puppy/Andrew Catterall), 44 (Castle on Lake Geneva/IMAGINA Photography), 45 (Mountain hiker/Melba Photo Agency), 47 (European brown bear/Arco Images GmbH), 51 (Market researchers/Detail Nottingham), 74 (housing development/Martin Shields); Corbis pp55 (Couple standing in kitchen/Solus-Veer), 56 (Primary school children in Kenya/Amanda Koster); DK Images pp12 (rucksacks/Andy Crawford); Getty Images pp8 (man leaning at bar/Christopher Leggett), 9 (portrait of young woman smiling/Juho Kuva), 24 (couple in kitchen/Allen Simon), 28 (state visit at Buckingham Palace/Tim Graham Photo Library), 34 (Couple sheltering from rain under map/Bob Elsdale), 35 (Actor Arnold Schwarzenegger at film premiere/AFP), 37 (quartz crystal skull/AFP), 48 (mature businessmen/Emmanuel Faure), 57 (Aral Sea desert/Karen Kasmauski), 60 (rainy day/Fred Paul), 62 (man laden with shopping bags/Jim Naughten), 65 (Senior man holding cup of coffee/Ulrika Finnberg), 68 (Minneriya National Park Sri Lanka/Jason Edwards); Kobal Collection p27 (Flightplan/Touchstone); OUP pp47 (Man wearing headset/Stockbyte), 60 (friends chatting/Corbis); Photolibrary pp12 (magnifying glass/F Schussler/PhotoLink), 12 (pocket knife/Thomas Northcut), 30 (Thieves robbing bank/Radius Images), 37 (two women in a cafe/Corbis), 53 (woman having hair done/Steve Levine), 61 (laptop in business case/Ryan McVay); PunchStock pp 4 (couple relaxing in a tent/Somos), 12 (ladder/fStop), 19 (university students on campus/fStop), 32 (Laboratory technicians/Imagemore), 47 (learning to skateboard/Hola Images), 65 (man in limousine/Digital Vision); Retna Pictures Ltd p23 (Freddie Mercury/Mick Rock).